LAND
of
SNOW
&
ASHES

LAND
of
SNOW
&
ASHES

Petra Rautiainen

Translated from the Finnish by David Hackston

PUSHKIN PRESS

Pushkin Press
71–75 Shelton Street
London WC2H 9JQ

Original text © Petra Rautiainen 2020
English translation © David Hackston 2022

First published in 2020 by Otava Publishing Company as *Tuhkaan piirretty maa*

Published in the English language by arrangement with Rights & Brands

First published by Pushkin Press in 2022

This work has been published with the financial assistance
of FILI – Finnish Literature Exchange

FILI
FINNISH
LITERATURE
EXCHANGE

1 3 5 7 9 8 6 4 2

ISBN 13: 978-1-78227-736-1

Designed and typeset by Tetragon, London

Printed and bound by CPI Group (UK) Ltd, Croydon, CRO 4YY

www.pushkinpress.com

LAND

of

SNOW

&

ASHES

I

INARI

Feb. 1944

I ARRIVED in Inari yesterday, transferred from the penal colony at Hyljelahti. This new camp isn't marked on Finnish maps. It lies about twenty kilometres to the north-east of Inari parish church. The lake is nearby. There is no proper road to speak of, and as you turn towards the camp two large trees hide everything from view. By the trees there are a couple of sign-posts informing us in German and Inari Sámi that trespassing is punishable by death—Sámi because anyone hiking around here is likely a Lapp trekking across the fells. Whether or not they can read is anybody's guess.

Hänninen was there to meet me. I introduced myself: Väinö Remes, martial official, interpreter. He said nothing, sized me up from head to toe. I imagine I must have looked quite young. We drove along the footpath in a German vehicle. At first the guard on duty didn't react at all, but when he saw the officer his expression changed. You could see from the young German's eyes that he was afraid. On one side of his collar was the insignia of a skull. Hänninen said something and offered him a cigarette. The guard declined. I'm not sure whether he understood any Finnish.

Hänninen explained the same things I already knew. Just as before, the prisoners are segregated into different tents. The

9

tent on the left is for Ukrainians, the next one along for Soviets and the one after that for Serbs. And there is a fourth tent here too. He didn't tell me anything about that one. I don't know what is in there.

There are no Jews here. Any Jews, or suspected Jews, are transferred to the penal colony at Hyljelahti. There aren't as many prisoners here as there are elsewhere, but more arrive in a continuous stream. According to Hänninen, another consignment of prisoners came by ship from Danzig the day before yesterday, among them Poles and Romanians. From tomorrow they will be set to work building the road to the north. There are a few other camps nearby, one of which is reserved for Germans, race traitors and those convicted of treason. Every Sunday they are rounded up and taken to the county jail in Inari for execution.

You cannot describe this camp without mentioning the smell. The fresh winter air notwithstanding, the stench of death hangs all around. The smell struck me in the face as Hänninen pushed open the door of one of the tents. Right in the middle of the tent, amid a clutter of dirty blankets, stood a strange-looking contraption. I don't know why, but at first I thought it must have been a rubbish bin made of old tin cans. You can make all kinds of things out of tin, but I soon realized that the assemblage in fact served as a small stove. The men slept tight together, some chained to the tent's iron structure and the rest shackled to one another. There was no fire in the stove, though it was freezing cold. The stench coming off the prisoners was so repulsive that I broke out in a coughing fit.

Hänninen told me that people get used to the smell. His eyes were languid and sleepy. I know where a look like that comes from. I asked him why there was no fire in the prisoners' stove. He replied that yesterday one of the prisoners had brought firewood into the tent without permission.

We continued on our way to a building standing next to a trench cut into the peat, its colourless walls made from long-dead pine trees and with only two windows. Inside the building it was warm. Hänninen stepped into the room and logged my arrival by noting the details in a ledger. I signed the page without reading what it said, and he didn't look at what I wrote either. He's fed up with all this too.

Hänninen impressed upon me that I should always follow orders and that I am here to serve the Germans, not only as an interpreter but also as a guard. He told me the story of another guard, Lars something or other, who had inadvertently leant so far into the guard's booth that he couldn't be seen from afar. Commander Felde, who was to be my superior, had just returned to the camp, drunk, after a meeting with provincial governor Hillilä and Colonel Willamo. He shot the guard on the spot. Hänninen said he had witnessed it himself. He had been with the commander at the time, claimed he still had bits of the boy's brain spattered on his shirt collar. As he told me all this he took something small from the upper shelf, stuffed it in his pocket, then picked up his suitcase from the floor.

Once outside, he handed me my weapons and various other accoutrements. A rifle and a pistol. It was the first time I had ever carried anything like this. In my previous roles, I had had neither permission nor inclination to bear arms. The pistol belt felt surprisingly heavy. We walked in silence towards the guard's booth, where I was due to start a shift. Before we parted ways,

Hänninen took a brown-glass phial from his pocket, a blank label attached to its side. He administered a few drops into his mouth, swallowed and cleared his throat. He looked at me closely, as though he was about to ask if I was cold. I tugged instinctively at my thick coat, beneath which I had pulled on an extra overcoat, and wiggled my toes inside my oiled and waterproofed boots.

Hänninen took his watch from his pocket, glanced at it and wound it up, then gazed at the sky. 'There's a Finnish prisoner here too,' he all but whispered, and I didn't have the chance to ask anything further before he wished me good luck and retraced his own steps back through the gates, walked to the car and slammed the black door shut behind him. The rear lights flared red as a German guard stepped out of the booth, stood to attention and headed back to his barracks for the night. Then I took his place.

It was around three-fifteen in the morning when I saw a solitary shooting star fall from the sky. But I didn't dare make a wish.

This land can no longer afford wishes.

This is a lost land.

ENONTEKIÖ, 1947

I T WAS FIVE TO ELEVEN when Inkeri parked her car outside the Falun-red house. The sun had dipped beneath the fells, casting shadows across the glistening surface of the lake behind the house. There was no road up to the house, only a semblance of a path, which meant Inkeri had to park her car some distance from the front steps. She examined the house through the dusty windscreen, hardly able to see a thing. She was carrying a photograph, the same one upon which she had based the decision to buy the house, and now she tried to compare the image to what she saw in front of her. She bit her lip and lowered the photograph. Her eyes moved from the house to the ball of white fur, which now seemed to glow golden as it dangled from the rear-view mirror. Inkeri stroked it with her forefinger. *We're here*, she whispered to the trinket, gave a wan smile and took off her round black sunglasses. Her eyes ached, stung. She wished she was somewhere else.

The journey from Helsinki had been a long one. Besides the fact that it had taken her many days, Inkeri had been forced to stop several times to calm her breathing. The roads were in bad condition; in places they were downright life-threatening. Vehicles careered here and there, their drivers apparently uninterested in whether or not they were fit to drive when they sat behind the wheel. Though seemingly innocuous, the dust was worst of all. Inkeri had seen a lot of sand in Africa. She had experienced the aridity, the strong winds. She had witnessed extraordinary sandstorms, one of which, in 1932, had proved fatal for several workers on their plantation. She had learnt that sand can be dangerous. She knew that when ground to a powder, these tiny grains can force their way in through your nose and ears. She knew how they dried the eyes, and at worst they could leave you with the perpetual sensation of having something stuck in the eye. Inkeri knew that sensation only too well. But she hadn't imagined experiencing the same thing here. An almost invisible dust had engulfed her on all sides, causing uncontrollable coughing fits. Even the oranges she had brought from Sweden had turned grey after a few hours' driving through the Lappish terrain. It was only later that she realized the dust might in fact be ash.

Inkeri rubbed her eyes and focused her gaze on the house. To her surprise, against the wall was a pig's feeding trough filled with flowers in an abundance of colours. She could hardly believe her eyes. On the journey here she hadn't seen any flowers at all, not so much as a dandelion. She tried to wipe the windscreen clean, but to no avail. She opened the car door and picked up her camera from the passenger seat.

Everything was quiet.

The leaves of the pansies, geraniums and other small flowers swayed gently in the wind. They were so beautiful that for a moment Inkeri forgot where she was and why. Then the smell of burnt kerosene flooded her nostrils. She placed her camera back on the seat, plucked a cigarette from her blouse pocket and took her hip flask from the glove compartment. After stepping out of the car, she took a swig and lit her cigarette. Somewhere nearby, a bird began singing. It was a common cuckoo, a male. Its song carried in from far across the still waters of the lake. An hour from now it would be midnight.

'What are you standing there for, letting the midges eat you alive?'

Inkeri jumped as she heard the rasping voice behind her.

'Sorry, didn't mean to startle you.'

The speaker chuckled, and she turned. Standing in front of her was a man of around seventy; Inkeri had checked his age on the deeds to the house. She pulled down the hem of her blouse and caught the bitter odour of sweat on the travel clothes she had had made in Sweden.

'Hello. I'm Inkeri. Inkeri Lindqvist,' she said and extended her hand.

'Ah, so you're Mrs Lindqvist. The new owner.' The man gripped her hand. He was wearing a blue Sámi hat, its peaked corners pointing in four directions. Inkeri had seen these hats on postcards designed for tourists.

'Piera's the name. Just fetching some water from the well.' Piera nodded behind him, where Inkeri saw a well standing in front of an old barn and the privy. Beside the well was a tree the colour of rust; Inkeri quizzically raised an eyebrow as she saw it. The man looked over his shoulder, then back at her.

'Folk around here think that tree must be growing right above a water vein, that's why it's so stunted. Half the house is in its path too, so you should sleep above a copper plate, if you believe in things like that.'

'I don't believe in things like that,' said Inkeri, lifting her chin.

'Good. Me neither,' said Piera happily and peered curiously at the hip flask. 'Is that real liquor you got there?'

'Yes, it's real,' said Inkeri. She looked first at the man, then her flask. 'Care for a sip?'

'I could have a dram. Haven't had proper stuff around here for years,' said Piera, reaching across to take the flask. 'Well. How was the journey? Many bodies by the roadside?'

Inkeri took a gulp from her flask and coughed. She nodded. Throughout the length of the journey, she had seen crosses erected along the sides of the roads, for people and for animals. She had seen at least three human bodies on the drive from Rovaniemi to Muonio, and countless dead reindeer, one of which was half eaten, the rest nothing but bones. They were everywhere. Bodies and mines.

Inkeri heard the front door opening. A youngish man stepped out of the dim interior and stood at the top of the steps. He put his hands in his pockets and observed them. Inkeri glanced at Piera, who had picked up a pail and was now walking past her. Only then did she notice that three fingers were missing from his left hand. The rest all looked blackened. Piera caught her staring at it.

'Lightning,' he said with a wink and popped his pipe in his mouth. Inkeri stared at him for a moment longer, then turned and looked at the younger man.

'And you must be Olavi. Olavi Heiskanen, yes?'

'I was about to go to sleep when I heard voices,' he said grumpily, and shook her hand.

'I see. I'm your new landlady. I understand you would like to remain living here as my tenant, even though I'll be living in the house too?'

'Yes, ma'am. If that's all right with you,' he said. They looked at each other for a moment. Olavi took a cigarette from his pocket, propped it between his lips, flicked a silver lighter and lit it. Inkeri did not reply.

'There's a shortage of housing around here. Buildings are only half finished. The war destroyed everything. There's no room for anybody. Even the Quakers who came from America earlier in the summer are still living in a tent. Piera will go and live with his son twenty-odd kilometres away. They've built a proper house.'

'That's right, I'll only be in your way tonight, I'm helping rebuild the church.' Piera clenched his pipe between his teeth and grinned. Inkeri raised a hand to shade her eyes from the midnight sun and studied both of them, scrutinizing the younger man from head to toe.

'It's fine. You can pay me the same rent you've been paying Piera,' she said. 'But I don't want anyone else living in the house. I need peace and quiet. And if living together causes any problems, we can talk about them and sort them out, yes?'

Olavi lowered his gaze; Inkeri thought she saw a hint of a smile. Then he nodded.

'Yes.'

Inkeri glanced at the trough and was about to comment on the flowers but lit another cigarette instead. If anything had ever grown in this land of dwarf birches, there was no longer any trace of it. The earth had been ravaged, scorched and destroyed. The trees had been felled during the war, and those that were left standing had eventually been burnt. Their gnarled skeletons dotted the edge of the road here and there, their thorny branches jutting ghost-like in all directions, charred and disjointed, like swords or sabres. Amid the desolation, chimney stacks stood tall, marking the spots where houses once stood. They too seemed to grow from the earth in curious, grotesque formations. Inkeri had heard that the Sámi people were unaccustomed to the newfangled ovens provided from the south, so after the war they had all wandered back to the remains of their own brick stoves like pilgrims.

'May I ask what you're doing here, ma'am?' Olavi asked.

'I've been commissioned to write news stories about the reconstruction of Lapland. This will soon be a modern place. The state is investing in the region very generously,' she explained. 'I intend to head up to the fells this week, weather permitting.'

'The fells?' asked Piera.

'Yes,' she said, and looked at him. 'I shall need a guide to show me all the little Lappish villages that are still standing. Would you come with me?' Piera raised his eyebrows.

'Stories about the modernization of Lapland and the disappearance of Sámi culture, eh?' Olavi smirked, his cigarette hanging from the corner of his mouth. 'The paper bought you an entire house for *that*?' There was an uncomfortable silence, during which Piera scuffed the grass with the tips of his boots.

'What about you, Olavi? Are you a local?'

'Me?' Olavi laughed, and looked up at Inkeri, amused. 'No, I'm not a local.'

'He's a southerner, all right,' Piera chuckled. 'Ovllá, we call him. Came up here at the end of the Continuation War, and he's been here ever since.'

'I'm helping to rebuild the church,' Olavi answered quickly, interrupting Piera.

'Ah yes, the building site I passed a kilometre or so down the road? It was hard to make head or tail of it, but I guessed it must be a church.'

'Yes.'

'And there were construction workers there too—at this time of the night,' said Inkeri, thinking of the burning mound she had passed. A fire was flickering in the church grounds. Maybe the workers had built a kiln to make charcoal or something similar. Inkeri had noticed that the men had rags wrapped round their feet. And all of a sudden, Kaarlo appeared in her mind. The thought came like a bolt of lightning or a sudden, heavy shower, just as it always did, right out of the beautiful, open, carefree sky. And it changed everything.

She looked around. This was the last place Kaarlo had been seen before he disappeared. She swallowed and tried to focus her thoughts on something else. The men asked whether she would like to come inside. Inkeri feigned a smile.

'Yes. Would you help me with the suitcases?' she stammered. Olavi and Piera picked up three suitcases each. Inkeri carried her camera.

As she stepped over the threshold, Inkeri could not help thinking about the men working at the church, the men with shoes made of soaked bark so that they could walk across the smouldering ground. She felt as though she were in exactly the same situation.

INARI

W E INTERPRETERS don't have huts of our own, as is the custom. Instead, here we live in barracks alongside the other guards and soldiers. At the previous camps I have visited I was largely left to my own devices, able to write my diary and read and talk only with those people I wished to, play chess and draughts. Here we all eat at the same time too.

In addition, the sleeping conditions are unbearable, and I find it hard to get any kip. The sheer number of men here creates an almighty stench. The bedframes creak at even the slightest movement. It repulses me to think how dirty this place is. Thankfully there are no lice, but I shave my body hair every morning as a precaution and keep my hair cropped short. The German lad on the next bunk along told me he melts candlewax and uses that to strip off all his body hair. All of it. I am unsure whether this is true or not, and I don't wish to find out.

I have been given a new interview jotter with a blue cover. Whenever I start an interview, I place the pad of squared paper on the desk, slightly to my right, and line up two pencils and a rubber next to it. I don't know why, but the women are always the last to be interviewed. Perhaps it is because some of them are then sent to the kitchen or the infirmaries, some even go to work for the provincial doctor. After each interview I erase from the jotter any sections deemed irrelevant as per our instructions. Sometimes it is easiest simply to burn entire pages.

Today was tough. I conducted ten hours of interviews in a row, with only one break, and even that I spent smoking a cigarette.

Feb. 1944

Felde introduced himself to me today. He is the one in charge around here and under whose directives I must operate. He sat with his feet propped on the desk, leafing through my papers. I told him who I am and reeled off my titles. I was surprised to hear him speak Finnish. Perhaps he learnt it from one of the local whores. There are plenty of them around here. Young girls from the cities in the south, some barely twelve or thirteen, travel up north on freight trains to spread their legs, and they never return home again. They remain on this side of the northern border, wandering the streets in a drug- and alcohol-induced stupor, and those that don't die a violent death eventually end up at labour camps scattered across the country. Then they die there instead.

Commander Felde is surely the kind of man who has had his fair share of whores. He gave a dull, condescending laugh at my title. 'I say, martial official, no less.' The term was concocted in five minutes when the decision was reached to send Finnish interpreters and police officers to Nazi camps to work for the fatherland. The title hasn't been amended or clarified since, perhaps because we do not officially exist. Felde asked about my news and seemed particularly interested in my work at the paramilitary unit Einsatzkommando Finnland and at the Stalag 309 camp.

'Do you believe in a Greater Finland and the primacy of the Finnish race?'

'Yes, Commander, sir! It is imperative that we eradicate all foreign elements from among our Finnish brethren across the border so that our peoples may be properly educated and become upstanding citizens of a Greater Finland!' I shouted, foaming at the mouth, my back so straight that it hurt. Felde looked at me lethargically from beneath his furrowed brow. I could tell from his expression that he didn't trust me. It's hardly surprising. You shouldn't trust anybody, here or anywhere else. Particularly anywhere else.

The commander listed my duties, the guidelines and the rules within the camp. He emphasized that I now worked primarily for the Gestapo, not the state of Finland, and that if I ever had to contact the Finnish Security Police I would have to run all messages by him first. 'I don't want any Finnish spies lurking around,' he said slowly, his eyes fixed upon me. He reminded me that, just like everybody else, I was to keep an eye not only on the prisoners but on the other guards too. It seemed some of the guards had begun to treat the prisoners more leniently. The men had lost their resolve, their vigour.

'These days, all the men want is to go home,' he said. 'Back to Germany, to their wives and families.' If I noticed anything suspicious, I was to inform him without delay.

On the spur of the moment, I asked him about the other Finn at the camp. Felde nodded and looked pleasantly surprised. He began speaking about the man. Apparently, he studies theology and is a member of the Academic Karelia Society. I narrowed my eyes somewhat, wondering why he was talking about a prisoner in this manner. I asked what he meant.

'Yes, the other guard,' he said. 'The Finnish guard.' I was taken aback and asked whether there was another Finnish guard here as well.

'Yes, there is. His name is Olavi Heiskanen.'

ENONTEKIÖ, 1947

I NKERI SAT DOWN at the green-painted table in the living room and, using a pair of tongs, smoked a cigarette rolled in newspaper. The fragrance of summer was all around, everywhere save for her. After their excursion into the fells, the smell of moss and the Sámi huts had become ingrained in her clothes and skin. Her hands were stained from the ink and the roll of film, and she couldn't get the dirt off properly. Her armpit hair stank, and her shirt was yellowed with sweat from the trek, though she had washed it twice in the tiny outdoor sauna. In her previous life she could never have imagined setting foot in such a grubby place.

She had decided to set up a darkroom in a small closet off the hallway that had probably once been a pantry. It wasn't perfect, but it would have to suffice. At first glance, this was the only space in the house that would be suitable for her purposes. It had no windows, but light still seeped through the chinks between the wall panels. Something would have to be done about that. Inkeri was already impatient; she yearned for the smell of developer fluid and the feel of the cool rinsing solution between her fingers, selecting and measuring the photographic paper, then watching the image slowly appear on its surface. *Photography*. That unfathomable, beautiful, incredible thing. After all these years, she was still utterly enthralled by it.

Inkeri looked to her side. Olavi was sitting eating cake on her sofa, which was exactly where the driver from Eskelinen's delivery company had left it. Olavi was slurping coffee and leafing through an old newspaper, lost in thought. The two did not speak. Inkeri took a better grip of her tongs. She would have to get hold of some proper filters and cigarette papers. She was too old for this. She needed to get her hands not only on implements to smoke properly but to build her darkroom too. Photographic paraphernalia was already strewn across the table: a magnifying glass for the negatives, piles of different-sized photographic paper, bowls she had decided to use for the different fluids, and some punnets, clothes pegs, tweezers and protective glasses. And her cameras.

'Quite a collection you have there. Should help make the place feel cosier,' said Olavi, interrupting her reverie. He had noticed the pensive look on Inkeri's face.

'Didn't you bring anything here with you?'

Olavi shrugged his shoulders by way of a negative response.

'Nothing at all?' Inkeri asked, perplexed, and stubbed out her cigarette.

'I came straight from the war. All I had was a watch and the clothes I was wearing. And some tobacco.'

'What's that then?' Inkeri asked, and pointed at a folder lying on a small shelf. Olavi turned to look at it.

'A stamp collection, by the looks of it.'

'Yes, I know what it is,' she tutted. Since moving into the house, she had flicked through it every now and then. 'Isn't it yours?'

'No. It belongs to Piera.'

'Him?' Inkeri furrowed her brow.

'Yes.'

'But that folder has lots of fine stamps in it, some of them very valuable. Old stamps from Canada and Alaska. How did Piera get his hands on those?' Piera certainly didn't give the impression of being an ardent philatelist. Inkeri had finally convinced him to guide her through the fells, and after a little persuasion he had even agreed to be interviewed for her upcoming story. Inkeri didn't particularly enjoy the trip. The company was stoical and the cold tangible. Though it was the height of summer, some of the trees on the higher slopes hadn't yet come into bud. The hardiest of the flowers were small and had barely popped their heads above ground.

'Well, be that as it may…' Inkeri cleared her throat. 'Are you ready to go?'

Olavi nodded.

Inkeri leant across the table to gather her belongings, picked up the Contax camera and weighed it in her hand. She planned to write a piece about the laying of the church foundations and wondered what the most suitable instrument might be for the job, for this day, this light.

'Ah, yes!' she suddenly whooped. She opened the cupboard beneath the sink, took out a transparent bottle and held it out towards Olavi.

'Is that the real stuff or some old rotgut?'

'It's real liquor, all right,' she said with a smirk. Olavi's expression brightened in a flash.

They both quickly emptied their glasses, then licked their lips and stared at the floorboards. Inkeri's mind was a blank.

'Let's go,' she said eventually without looking up at Olavi. 'Let's go.'

Olavi pulled on his cap and picked up something wrapped in a cloth. Inkeri put on her sunglasses before they had even opened the door. The churchyard was a kilometre away. Inkeri and Olavi walked the distance without exchanging a word. Sunlight glinted here and there from between the clouds. Olavi noted Piera from a distance, and Inkeri followed him towards the old man. Piera was an easy man to spot. He was dressed in bright colours: the embroidered vertical ribbons on his back gleamed in the sunshine, and his silver-woven belt almost sparkled. The bright colours aside, he was still sporting those brown-tanned reindeer-hide trousers, the same ones he had been wearing on their little trip up into the fells. Piera had taken Inkeri along the ancient herding routes and brought her to the traditional *siida* where his family lived during the summer months, just as she had asked. There were fewer than ten inhabitants in the village. The Sámi huts were dotted sparsely. The women scythed hay for the villagers' shoes and the men went fishing. The children played. The smell of smoke seemed like a faint reminder of a bygone age. Inkeri had begun writing the article, but it wasn't yet complete and later in the autumn she planned to develop it into a larger, two-page spread.

'… and we played at herding and throwing the lasso…' Inkeri heard a girl dressed in a bright-red cap telling Piera. The girl was holding a curiously shaped wooden block.

'What's that?' Inkeri asked, interrupting the girl's story. The girl smiled. There was a small gap between her front teeth.

'It's an *áldu*,' said the girl. 'In Finnish it's called a *vaami*. I'm Bigga-Marja.'

'*Vaami*?'

'That's right. Don't you know what a *vaami* is? It's a reindeer doe,' she said, and looked keenly at Inkeri's camera. 'And what's that?'

'This is a camera. Don't you know what a camera is?' said Inkeri. 'I write pieces for the newspaper. I'm a reporter,' she explained. She took off her sunglasses and closed her eyes for a moment. 'Perhaps I could interview you too.' The girl first looked puzzled, then gave a nod. She began answering Inkeri's questions carefully but with great enthusiasm. In her quick, messy hand, Inkeri wrote down that Bigga thought the new church was a good thing because the temporary church was terrible. 'But not as terrible as the temporary schools and hostels,' she muttered, lowering her eyes and hiding behind Piera. She gave a shy smile, her front teeth resting on her lower lip. Inkeri raised her eyes.

'The hostels?'

'Yes. I live in a hostel,' said Bigga, and turned her head towards the school, next to which stood a row of dormitories. For a moment they all looked at the buildings in silence, then Inkeri turned her attention back to the girl. She had long fair hair and dark eyes, set deep in their sockets. A curious-looking silver ball dangled from her belt.

'And where have you learnt such good Finnish?' When she had been out talking to the locals, she hadn't encountered a single person who spoke Finnish—or who agreed to speak it to her, that is.

'Of course I speak Finnish. I'm eleven already,' said Bigga, her chin high and proud.

'Bigga-Marja was evacuated during the war, like so many of the children,' Piera explained. 'Her mother died of a chest infection that was going around. Her father, my son, died in the war. Bigga was in Vittangi, on the Swedish side, but the children learnt all kinds of things there. Even Finnish.' From Piera's tone of voice, it was clear this was the end of the discussion.

'Is that so?' Inkeri closed her notepad and put away her pencil. She raised her camera to ask if she could take a photograph, and after a nod from Bigga she began to set up the camera.

'That isn't a traditional Sámi costume you have, is it?' Inkeri asked, and looked first at Bigga's dress then eagerly scrutinized Piera's attire, the colourful baize cloth and gleaming thread decorating his cap. 'Do you have a traditional Sámi costume? I'm sure my readers would like to see that.'

'I don't have a proper one.'

'Really?' said Piera. 'You just didn't want to put it on, more like.' When he spoke to the locals, Piera's speech seemed oddly slow. Inkeri had noted the way that different languages and vernaculars mingled throughout the churchyard. There were the Quakers with their accents from across the United States, there were the Sámi languages—until now, Inkeri hadn't appreciated how much they differed from one another—there was Norwegian and Swedish, and then there was Finnish, with dialects from every corner of the land.

Somewhat reluctantly, Piera and Bigga posed for a photograph. Inkeri focused her camera, adjusted the lens and clicked the shutter. The flash was unnecessarily bright, but they couldn't very well do without it. 'I should have taken this cap off too,' she heard Bigga complaining. Inkeri thanked them and went on her way.

Further off, near the foundations of the new church, someone had started giving a speech, and the others had gathered around to listen. Everyone except Inkeri. At moments like this, she was able to move through the throngs of people unnoticed. It was a peculiar feeling. It was as though people had frozen on the spot, as though she wasn't there at all.

She walked forwards, and before long she was right in the middle of a cluster of people. It seemed everybody really had turned up for the event. Those from Norway and Sweden were easily identifiable by their distinctive *gákti*, their traditional costumes. The embroidery on their headdresses was different too, the hats were sewn in a manner that Inkeri had never seen on the Finnish side of the border. Even the tassels were shaped differently. Their jewels and trinkets, charms and buckles jangled with every step.

Inkeri immersed herself in taking photographs. To her, photography was everything. When she examined objects through a lens, she felt as though she was in exactly the same place, every single time, regardless of where in the world she found herself, whether she was photographing a duke or a labourer on a plantation. Deep inside, she was always in the same spot. Nothing else had any meaning. She had fallen in love with photography as a child, when she had touched her family's old wooden camera for the first time and examined family photographs preserved in a heavy, locked album. Portraits from the atelier, scenes of people taking afternoon coffee in Sinebrychoff Park.

Photographs of vast rooms, light streaming in through their windows, where the plants stood so tall that they touched the ceiling. In these images she had seen people, rooms, scenarios about which she wanted to know more, to tell more.

And when, as a younger woman, Inkeri had been offered an apprenticeship at the atelier, she had finally allowed herself to dream that perhaps she too might one day earn a living as a photographer. She had even joined the Finnish Photographers' Association. But after a promising start, over the years Inkeri came to realize that the path for a female photographer was a very narrow, arduous one. She was destined to remain an atelier photographer, taking portraits and contrived indoor scenes, though she wanted to do precisely the opposite.

The sun peered out from behind a cloud. Inkeri's head began to ache instantly. Without even noticing, she had strayed further away from the crowd. The brightening of the sun meant she would have to adjust the exposure time. She lifted the camera up to her eye and was about to refocus when, from the blur of the lens, Olavi appeared, standing next to the church foundations. She lowered the camera, looked around and raised it again. As she focused the lens, she saw that Olavi was taking out an object wrapped in a cloth.

The object glinted in his hand.

Inkeri watched as he lowered the object into the foundations, leaving it there to be bricked away for ever, before disappearing back into the crowds. She waited for a moment, then strolled up to the foundations and walked around until she reached the spot where Olavi had been standing only a moment ago. She had guessed right. It was a photograph. She raised the photograph to eye level and felt suddenly faint. A moment later, she pulled a cigarette from her jacket pocket and stood smoking it pensively.

During her time in the savannah, Inkeri had learnt that there is rarely a time when animals are truly at rest. But when the rainy season started, when after a long, deathly arid period the animals were able to drink their fill of water, that was when the miracle really happened. Lions, flamingos, African roller birds, monkeys and buffalos, all side by side drinking from the same riverbed. At the same time. The birds perched on the backs of the lions, giraffes and rhinoceroses, all twittering, carefree.

Inkeri gazed at the panorama in front of her. Two months ago she had heard that, during the war, there used to be a prison camp somewhere nearby. She glanced once more at the photograph, stubbed out her cigarette, looked furtively around and quickly slipped the frame under her arm. If there were only scant moments of peace in the savannah, elsewhere in the world there were even fewer.

INARI

Feb. 1944

TODAY I SAW Olavi Heiskanen for the first time, when the guards returned with a small group of prisoners from the road construction site. Most of the prisoners spend their days at labour camps or construction sites across the province, some of them even beyond the old border. Olavi Heiskanen held out his hand and introduced himself. He seems jovial, a young man around my age. Light-brown hair, no beard. Large blue eyes. The Finnish prisoner or menial, the one I'd heard about earlier, was with him. Later on, I learnt that the two spend all their time together. If one of them is off working somewhere, the other will always be nearby. The Finnish prisoner was nondescript, he stood somewhat hunched, he was a scrawny, bearded man in his forties or fifties. He doesn't speak to me, and I don't address him.

Heiskanen tells me this prisoner is known simply as Kalle. But I still haven't quite established why the man is here at all. Perhaps he was a communist during the Civil War, one of many who fled to the Soviet Union and was now pretending to be a real Finn. Who knows? I did learn, however, that he lives in a tent reserved for the trusted prisoners.

There is something untoward about this Kalle. He is allowed

to move around relatively freely; just now he was humming along to a *Schlager* song on the Lapplandsender forces wireless and went into the barn to take care of the animals without asking permission. Nobody did anything. Even Felde walked past without paying the infraction any attention.

And on top of that, at supper this evening I saw there was an extra potato on his plate.

Feb. 1944

Heiskanen helps me with my interpreting tasks and in taking measurements. When new consignments of prisoners arrive, we check their background and define their race, we separate any non-desirable elements, which are eliminated as need be, and make a note of any new arrivals that might be valuable for intelligence purposes.

Kalle speaks a great many languages, including Polish, English and French, and even a few rare African Bantu tongues. We ask him to help us as required. Sometimes there is nothing to do, and Kalle spends his time playing with the cat. All the same, he is very useful indeed. With his help, we can gain a better understanding of precisely which nationalities have been sent here. And he helps with the measuring too. Whenever the doctor is here with his assistant, the measuring is his job; at other times it is our responsibility. I have never done a job like this before, and I find it revolting. The stink of the Soviet prisoners is unbearable, even after they have been washed and scrubbed. We measure the width of the head, examine the condition of the genitalia and note whether they have a foreskin or not. Heiskanen and I log all this information in the ledger.

I asked Heiskanen why Kalle is here at the German camp instead of one of the Finnish camps, like the one at Nastola— or Parkkina, perhaps, where the Finnic peoples, such as the Savakko, Äyrämöinen and Finnish Ingrian tribes, and former communists are re-educated into upstanding citizens, to provide a population and workforce for the Greater Finland of the future. Kalle is clearly well educated, and there is something almost aristocratic in his clear diction, his good manners and the way he carries himself.

'What kind of future are we living for?' Heiskanen answered my question, somewhat amused. Naturally, I replied by repeating what I had read long ago on page seven of the Academic Karelia Society magazine. I had torn out that page and glued it to the wall in the old privy. Heiskanen did not respond, and since then he has not really spoken to me.

Feb. 1944

There is a doctor here who visits regularly. I saw him this morning, then once again almost immediately during a cigarette break. He was standing in front of his shack, his head lowered. When he saw me, he peered at me for a long time before raising his hand. I think it must be because my uniform doesn't bear any skulls or other SS insignia. Heiskanen told me that the doctor is seconded here from Inari parish for one week at a time. He visits the camp once a month, distributes rubber prophylactics to the soldiers and checks for venereal disease. He conducts inspections and examinations of the prisoners too. Some of our new interviewees have to be taken directly to the doctor.

This afternoon the doctor gave the guards an educational talk about such diseases in the large hall. He told us how to clean the pee hole properly and explained how to take care of our personal hygiene in general, then reminded us that if we do start to show symptoms of any diseases, treatment is free of charge. He had with him a stick about twenty centimetres long. He held it up and said that anyone with suspected gonorrhoea would have this stick inserted into their member. This was presumably supposed to serve as a warning, but someone made a lewd comment, and of course everyone in the room burst into laughter. Everyone except the doctor. I haven't seen him smile once.

A woman arrived with the doctor. I understand she is a shamanistic bloodletter. A witch. *Noaidi*, in the local tongue. For some reason she is here working as a nurse. She didn't say anything to us and got straight to work. But I did catch sight of her eyes. They are a strange colour. I have never seen anything like it. I was afraid to look into them but couldn't help myself. They were like freshly blossomed heath violets or fat bilberries glistening in the morning dew. Not quite blue, but something altogether different.

A hue reflecting the piercing Arctic light and the universe.

ENONTEKIÖ, 1947

T HE KEY TO THE NEW school building was attached to a
keyring fashioned from a reindeer antler. A groove had
been carved into the keyring; it could have meant anything,
but in this instance it designated a number. 'Number one is the
master key,' Kuusela, the headmaster, explained as he turned
the key in the front door. 'I carry this key everywhere,' he continued, and politely held the door open for Inkeri, allowing her
to slip inside. Mr Kuusela was wearing a plain brown blazer
and a tie. His trousers were neatly pressed, and his hat smelt
of talcum powder.

Mr Kuusela was a small, rotund man. He took off his hat to
reveal a bald patch right in the middle of his head. His green-
rimmed spectacles kept slipping down the bridge of his nose.
He smiled a lot and exuded the kind of warmth that Inkeri
had always envied. She herself felt incapable of such a thing.
She had always found it hard to empathize with other people.

Kuusela showed her around the classrooms, gesturing right
and left. His words echoed through the empty building. Classes
had begun last week. It was Sunday, and there was nobody
else in the school. The previous week, Inkeri had attended the
school's opening festivities and arranged an interview with
Kuusela for today. She had written down in advance all the

things she wanted to ask him, but now none of these questions seemed to interest her. She had been unable to dispel the image of the photograph she had taken from the church's foundations. The photograph showed two soldiers. One of them was wearing the standard uniform of a Finnish private, but the other was dressed in full Nazi attire. From the stripes on his lapels and his general appearance, Inkeri presumed he must have been a high-ranking officer. Between the soldiers stood an older woman in Sámi apparel, smiling broadly at the camera. Sitting down was a doctor in a white coat, and beside him a dark-haired woman was perched on a branch, leaning forwards. It was hard to estimate her age, but she couldn't have been especially young either.

Inkeri was unsure whether the photograph had been taken in a genuine situation or whether it had been posed. Her experience suggested the latter, but the younger woman's expression made her doubt her instincts. If the image had been posed, it seemed the woman had been unable to hide her true emotions. There was something arresting in her gaze. Perhaps it was fear. Perhaps disgust. Whatever it was, it was something profound, something it was hard for Inkeri to look at. Something that made the image remarkable, extraordinary.

When she worked at the atelier, Inkeri had quickly become bored with staging prim-and-proper portraits and had started trying to incorporate into her photographs the kind of things that other studio photographers would have considered flaws. Symmetry should never be broken, and if it was, it had to be offset with another element, a hat or some kind of prop. To Inkeri, the flaws were the heart of the image. When she left the atelier and set off with Kaarlo to Kenya, the East African British colony, she was finally able to photograph mundane things and real, everyday people. Kenya was a country about which she hadn't heard a single word, but going there was one of the main reasons why she had accepted Kaarlo Lindqvist's proposal of marriage. She would be able to maintain her own freedom and continue working with her beloved photography. During her time in Kenya, Inkeri learnt that the local tribes believed the camera could snatch away their soul. Although this couldn't possibly happen, Inkeri had to admit that, on some level, she shared this notion. Ultimately, photography was about power; it was a type of manipulation.

However, neither the Nazi officer nor the woman sitting on the branch of the tree were the reason Inkeri had kept Olavi's photograph. In addition to these people, two other men appeared in the picture. Prisoners of war, of that there could be no doubt. Their gaunt faces and tattered clothes said as much. Why did Olavi possess a photograph like this in the first place? Inkeri had wondered whether to ask him about the picture or whether to forget all about it. She had decided to let the matter drop. For the time being, this was the safest option. After all, what did she really know about Olavi?

'These last few years, the children have attended classes at the temporary town hall. Of course, having our own school building is an enormous enhancement. As you can see, every-thing is new and pristine.' Kuusela cleared his throat. Inkeri caught the smell of freshly cut wood. Why did wood and grass smell so good the very moment after they had been through the chopper? Their steps echoed along the corridor and eventually came to an end in front of a classroom Kuusela had selected. He turned the key in the lock.

'This must all look very modest to a lady from the capital who has travelled the world, but it's a vast improvement on what we had before.' Kuusela laughed, opened the classroom door, stepped inside and sat at the teacher's table. Inkeri sat down at one of the pupils' desks. 'The school was built by the same architecture students who designed the new hotel at Pallas.' Bright light shone through the windows. There was no dust in sight.

'Would you tell me what you think about the current education system?' asked Inkeri, her words echoing around the empty classroom.

'Well. I certainly believe that the measure of a civilized society must be the quality of its schools,' he replied hazily, lifting his spectacles with the edge of his forefinger. 'Now we are finally able to provide both the Laplanders and the Sámi children with a decent education. In the past, this responsibility lay largely with a handful of travelling teachers. Now we have two new teachers, one of them from the Quaker community.'

Inkeri looked out of the window.

'This peripatetic missionary education has been stopped now, and teachers no longer travel out to the more remote villages. Whereas in the past these children were able to continue living up in the fells, now they are required by law to attend a proper school,' he explained, carefully watching Inkeri's reaction, which remained somewhat lacklustre.

'Education is the foundation of everything else,' she agreed, still gazing out at the church construction site opposite.

'Precisely, Miss Lindqvist, you're quite right! The matter of educating the Sámi is something that has caused particular concern and discussion.'

'Mrs.'

'Pardon me?'

'It's Mrs Lindqvist,' said Inkeri, and looked him in the eye. Mr Kuusela returned her gaze, somewhat befuddled, his eyes instinctively edging towards the ring finger on Inkeri's left hand. She felt embarrassed. She shouldn't have taken off her ring. She should have kept it.

'I am… Well, my husband is missing. Presumed dead,' she explained, and watched Kuusela's face fall. Inkeri observed him intently. There it was again. That same expression, as though she had suddenly turned into some fragile object. A moment later, Kuusela did something that was doubtless supposed to provide both comfort and support. He placed his hand on hers. Inkeri pulled back her hand and kept it in her lap. She hated gestures like these. What was one supposed to do? Was she expected to say, *it's nothing really*, or *everything will be fine*? Which of them would draw comfort from such words? Besides, who said she needed to be comforted?

'May I ask how your husband disappeared?'

'In the war, Mr Kuusela. He disappeared during the war,' she said through gritted teeth. He gave an empathetic nod, lowered his head and was silent for a moment.

'Well then…' he continued. 'The worrying situation is that most of these local children cannot speak Finnish when they first start attending school. They must be taught Finnish from scratch. Some pick it up rather quickly, while others, however…

41

The situation is hardly helped by the fact that the pupils usually continue to speak Sámi to one another outside the classroom. Many of the poor things walk kilometres simply to come to school, they live in extremely unpleasant conditions, and naturally this is reflected in their behaviour and such.' Kuusela rounded off his words with a curt nod. Inkeri looked at his head, his thinning tufts of hair, whipped by the elements.

'Tell me about the boarding pupils.'

'Indeed, many of them live in the dormitory across the way,' said Kuusela, gesturing out of the window.

'Are all of the children orphans?'

'No, not all of them, of course. But some of them have such a long journey to school, twenty, thirty kilometres. The children can treat this place like home. It is the best place for a child, most certainly better for many of them than living at home. Here they have food, relatively clean clothes and a good roof over their heads.'

Inkeri leafed through her jotter, thoughtful but still somewhat irked.

'I am trying to write as wide-ranging an article about these school conditions as possible, and I have already contacted the Lapland education council. The chairman sent me a letter in which he described these dormitories as "dubious places". He thinks it unnatural that the children only see their parents twice a year, and he finds it problematic that the bonds between the children and their families and traditions become weaker over time.'

The headmaster looked at her.

'Those are his words,' she affirmed, and consulted her notes.

'What exactly are you trying to say?'

'I'm not trying to say anything,' said Inkeri, her voice steady as she tried to force a smile. 'I merely wish to hear whether you'd like to comment on the matter. What do you think? Is it a problem that the children are so far from home?'

'It is certainly true, Inkeri—may I call you Inkeri?' She raised an eyebrow, but Kuusela continued talking. 'It's true that the children find this a little traumatic, particularly when they first arrive. But on the other hand, it is precisely the fact that they are able to live in the dormitories that is so beneficial to them. For many Sámi children, the dormitory is the best possible place.'

Inkeri was silent. She leant backwards on her bench and waited. Sometimes silence was more effective than words, more pressing. Sometimes it could be more destructive than a scream. But Kuusela did not seem to appreciate this as, unfazed, he proceeded to ask: 'Is it true that you have taught children in Africa too?'

'Yes, in Kenya. I gave a few classes there when I was still young,' Inkeri explained, and recalled the Kikuyu children's primitive school building. Those children who were allowed to attend school sat on the ground. They had no pencils or paper. Only years later did they acquire desks and chairs. The money for such things generally came from the church, from Western aid organizations, and sometimes from a private benefactor. At the crucial phase of the harvesting season the children were working and unable to attend school, and during this time Inkeri went out to the fields, took photographs of the workers, the women, the men and children, all dressed in whatever was to hand, some wearing only loincloths, others a shirt and trousers, scarves tied round their heads, behind them the sun and the ochre desert, and beyond that the majestic figure of Mount Kenya.

'It would be an honour if you would teach here too now and then. Perhaps you could teach the children Finnish.'

Inkeri stared at Kuusela. 'Thank you. I'll think about it.'

'How did you end up in Africa?' he enquired.

'Through my husband.'

'Really?'

'He was a partner in a tobacco plantation. Kaarlo was interested in education too. He wanted to help the Africans to study, and he became headmaster of a local school. I always wanted to become a photographer.'

'And did you?'

Inkeri looked at the headmaster, then turned and stared out of the window towards the church.

'How long will it take to rebuild the church?' she asked. Kuusela followed her gaze and shrugged his shoulders.

'I don't know. Years, I imagine. The church is the foundation of everything. And one has to lay foundations properly.'

'Were you here during the war?'

'No, I was not.'

'I've heard there used to be a prison camp nearby. I wonder if you could tell me anything about it. I might even write an article on the subject,' Inkeri added quickly.

'I have no knowledge of anything like that,' Kuusela replied, genuinely confused. Inkeri nodded. She glanced down at her jotter and thought of Kaarlo. Her husband had once said something to her that she only fully understood once it was too late: *Learn to know what you want. After that, learn to demand it.* She nervously tapped her pencil against the desk.

'In fact,' she began, and moved the jotter to one side. 'Perhaps I could teach here after all.'

'Splendid!' Kuusela exclaimed. 'You could start with the Finnish classes—'

'But,' she said, brusquely interrupting him, 'I won't teach Finnish or mathematics. And I won't tell the pupils about Africa or about what it is like being a professional woman.' Her voice had a tone that she had learnt to use when she wanted something.

'What will you teach, then?' Kuusela asked, rather baffled. Inkeri thought of her atelier, the aroma of paints, watercolours seeping into the paper. She thought of layers of different colours, their surfaces, the feel of taking a palette knife and scraping at a blot of paint that had almost dried. The acrid scent of turpentine, the sharp chill of the outdoor air, the tingle in her numb fingers, the skim of ice in the pots.

'I want to teach art. And by that, I don't mean simple drawing classes,' she whispered. Bright light flowed in through the window, and she closed her eyes.

Art.

INARI

Mar. 1944

HEISKANEN AND KALLE follow me around everywhere I go. I'm not sure, but I get the impression they are watching me. We have been assigned to the same tasks. Heiskanen talks a lot. But in among all the prattle there are subtle enquiries that, at first, I do not answer at all. He tells me quite freely about his own experiences, seemingly unconcerned that his every word might reach Felde's ears. Perhaps he is testing me. Perhaps he and Felde are somehow colluding with each other. I think of what Commander Felde said: here, the guards keep an eye on one another too.

Still, I told him that after leaving Einsatzkommando Finnland, I remained in the area conducting reconnaissance missions, operating mostly for the Gestapo. Heiskanen asked what these missions entailed. The same as here, I told him. 'Typing up endless reports,' I smirked. Everything had to be produced in duplicate, with copies going both to the Gestapo and the Finnish Security Police. 'Here we don't send the FSP anything. Of course, we produce documents, but then we destroy them. If we don't destroy them, the FSP most certainly will,' said Heiskanen, and smacked his lips. I chuckled, and Heiskanen chuckled too. Then he slapped me on the back and said he was truly relieved that they had sent another Finn to the camp. 'These German guards can't cope with silence. Some of them can't bear the light, others can't bear the darkness. Four years we've endured this, one miserable day at a time,' he said. The light is to blame, apparently. For half the year there is too much of it and for the other half there is no normal light to speak of and the sky is filled with ever-stranger phenomena that can make people believe in pagan gods, the devil, anything at all.

'The Kraut's head can't take things like that,' Heiskanen claimed. Though at the beginning relations between the troops were good, now he said we needed some Finnish reinforcements to help settle any 'misunderstandings arising from cultural differences'.

Mar. 1944

Another large consignment of prisoners arrived yesterday. They have come all the way from Danzig, first by ship to Helsinki, where they are herded straight on to a train bound for Rovaniemi. Then from Rovaniemi they are brought up here in a truck. The trucks drive through villages and parishes I have never heard of. Finally they arrive here, at the edge of the earth. Here they will die.

Many of the prisoners in yesterday's shipment were wounded or otherwise injured. I was involved in performing the initial assessment and race evaluation. I wrote everything down. It's curious, but you can spot different races a mile off. And it's not just about looks, it's something else. Their appearance, their gait. Some of the prisoners were executed in the backyard straight away. We didn't bother to log them in the ledger. Those prisoners requiring immediate medical attention, surgery, the removal of a bullet or the amputation of a limb, are left to wait until the doctor or the bloodletter get here.

Among the prisoners there were a few of our peoples from across the border. Two Karelians, one Russian Skolt. These poor wretches have already been through enough living under the yoke of the Soviets. I plan to suggest to Commander Felde that they be transferred to the Finnish camps.

Mar. 1944

Some of the prisoners have put together a theatre group. They perform for the officers a few times a month. Today they have a rehearsal, and I am on duty for the rest of the evening.

The bloodletter strode across the yard in long steps, her head uncovered, and a hairpin fell from her hair to the ground. I saw it because the sun was shining at just the right angle, making it sparkle. I looked for it in the snow but couldn't find it anywhere.

Mar. 1944

Rehearsals have been going well. There are ten members in the theatre group, and not all of them are trusted prisoners. The minute the door closed behind us, it almost felt as though we weren't at the camp at all. You notice that the prisoners have a hierarchy all of their own. A couple of them got into an argument about the main role. The leading actor died the other night of consumption, and the part had to be recast, but nobody seemed up to the job. The show is in a week's time. Eventually, the role was given to an elderly man who already walks with a stoop. I don't know how such a hunchback was ever sent to the front in the first place. He is suspected of being a Jew, so we have been told to keep an eye on him.

When he dies, his body will be sent to Germany for examination. If probability is anything to go by, it will happen sooner rather than later.

Mar. 1944

I have had a look at Kalle's identity card. His full name is Kaarlo Lindqvist, so he must be Finland-Swedish. Apart from this, his card is empty. No annotations whatsoever, not even the date of his arrest. No information about his state of health, his race. It's almost as though he is not a prisoner at all.

Kalle is treated better than all the other prisoners, and this special dispensation goes far beyond his extra potato. For instance, only yesterday the guards shot two passers-by who, as far as I could see, were simply walking back from the washroom to the barracks. Later on, I learnt that they had refused to wash because it was too cold. That is certainly true, as it's almost forty degrees below freezing. Regardless of the temperature, all prisoners are made to wash outdoors, their upper bodies bared to the elements. All except Kaarlo Lindqvist.

ENONTEKIÖ, 1947

As he arrived at the church construction site one bitter early autumn morning, Olavi noted two things: a shaggy creature was sniffing loudly around the site and a large flock of children were throwing a ball in front of the church. He recognized Bigga-Marja standing somewhat further off. 'Ovllá, come and play!' she called to him, bouncing her brown-leather ball up and down. There was banging and shouting all around, the snorting of horses. The air smelt fresh and pure.

'What are you playing?'

'*Spábbadoaškuma*,' Bigga-Marja cried.

'The flying ball?' Olavi asked, confused.

Bigga laughed and smirked at him. 'During the evacuation we used to play football, but this is really something!'

'Football, indeed…' Olavi looked closely at Bigga. Her fair hair stood on end, as if it were electrified, exactly as it had done in the autumn of 1944, just before the end of the war, when he had seen her for the first time. Tired and feverish, he had clambered out of the car and caught sight of Bigga-Marja standing in front of the house. She had been dressed in a pair of torn fur boots and traditional blue Sámi attire, the like of which Olavi hadn't seen her wearing since. Behind her was a clamour of smoke and fire. Olavi couldn't remember anything else. At that point, there was a gap in his memory. No, gap was the wrong word for what he had experienced. What he saw was emptiness, smoke and soot, he saw birds that had fallen to the ground. In mid-flight, just like that. They lay on the ground, charred, black as coal. Lifeless.

He and Bigga-Marja had never spoken about that time, but it shimmered between them every time they met. He knew it. Bigga-Marja knew it too.

The war had ended on the same day as he arrived in Enontekiö. Right across the province, the authorities began to clear the prison camps. Originally, he had intended to continue on his way and not stay here, but somehow things had turned out differently.

Olavi snapped out of his thoughts when a pig suddenly grunted between them. Bigga-Marja had crouched down to stroke it. The creature had a long woollen coat; it was almost the size of a sheep and looked like one too. Piera had named it Matilda after reading in the periodical about a British woman by that name who had travelled by herself to the ends of the earth. *Just like this here pig*, he had explained to Olavi. Piera thought it a noteworthy event, giving the pig an honorary moniker. Olavi knelt down to scratch the creature. Her little tail wagged like a dog's. And as Matilda was here, it meant that Piera was probably down at the worksite. Olavi found it all very strange. When Piera gave up his house he'd given up the smithy as well, so he no longer had any work to speak of. Dragging Matilda the pig twenty kilometres felt strange too, though they sometimes used her to look for mines or bodies. During the war—and afterwards—they had even used her to track down fugitives.

'Where's your cap?' Olavi asked Bigga. She quickly tucked her straggly hair away behind her ears.

'Somewhere…' she muttered, fidgeting with the small decorative ball dangling from her belt. The cradle-ball.

'Well, I'd best be getting to work, to build this *splendid new church…*' Olavi winked at her. 'Have you read the paper yet? Your picture is in there too.'

'No! Where can I see it?'

Olavi took the paper from his back pocket and opened it at the right page. Bigga-Marja stepped closer. It was a long article, mostly about how this new church would be the finest in the country and explaining that the locals had received help all the way from America. The organ pipes were to be built in Germany. The article was very flattering, though after writing it Inkeri had asked him how it was possible that these nomadic peoples, who wandered the fells and lived in a kind of isolation one could barely imagine, believed in the same God and that the locals were now building them the most beautiful church the country had ever seen. Inkeri had told him that in Helsinki, a thousand kilometres to the south, the Great Cathedral rose up into the blackening sky like a white dove, and explained that when you saw that dome, you saw the light.

She had experienced it herself.

To Olavi, the church was simply a building, a large room, nothing more.

Bigga quietly pored over the newspaper.

'Well?'

'Is that what I look like?' she asked eagerly.

'More or less. It's just a picture. You look different from different angles.'

'I'd like to take photographs too,' Bigga quickly added. 'It seems fascinating.'

Olavi adjusted his hat and folded up the newspaper. He lit a cigarette, but the girl didn't show any intention of leaving. Bigga looked down towards the provisions tent. Some of the Quakers had set up a group whose job it was to look after the children and cook porridge, as an emergency measure for those families who couldn't afford to feed their large broods. Another group took care of the entertainment. And there were lots of children. Some of them appeared malnourished, one or two of them were missing a leg, a third wore an eye patch. All had either been orphaned or came from a family that was unable to care for them. Olavi glanced at Bigga-Marja, who was staring at the canteen staff.

'Is it true that Inkeri used to live in the black man's land?' asked Bigga inquisitively. Olavi slipped his lighter back into his jacket pocket and allowed his eyes to alight on a dark-skinned woman whose hair curled from under her headscarf. 'Is she from Africa too? The Ivory Coast?' Bigga continued, now whispering.

'What do you know about the Ivory Coast?' Olavi chuckled. He caught the smell of porridge. When the foreign aid workers had arrived in Lapland, all questions about Olavi's background had suddenly come to an end. It was a relief. It was the first time any of them had ever seen a black person. As an object of curiosity, Olavi was far less interesting than these degenerates. That's what people would have said before and during the war, and such sentiments certainly hadn't disappeared, though now they were deemed inappropriate. *Well, I've seen it all now,* some joker chortled with a nod at the black Quakers. *Is that what they mean by a Greater Finland?*

'It's called the Ivory Coast because there's lots of ivory. People collect it, load it on to ships and send it to America. Is that where Inkeri was too?'

'Yes, she has been to Africa,' said Olavi.

'Have you heard she's going to start giving us art classes?' Bigga asked. 'Is that why she bought Áddjá's house?'

Olavi looked at Bigga and wondered what to say.

'I heard she's built a *sevdnjes lanja,* a room that's completely dark,' Bigga muttered. 'What's it for?'

'That's right,' Olavi began. 'It's for developing photographs.' Olavi hadn't visited Inkeri's darkroom, but he assumed the only light in there was a dim red glow and that otherwise it was pitch-dark. He couldn't say anything else about it, except that Inkeri had trodden all over his flowerbeds while she was blocking up the gaps in the outer wall. He'd felt peeved about it for days. He still was.

'Can I come and look at it sometime?' asked Bigga. Olavi flicked his cigarette to the ground.

'Put on your cap, so you don't catch your death,' he mumbled. Bigga-Marja replied with a smirk, snatched up the ball and ran off across the yard. The cradle-ball dangling from her belt jangled against her thigh. But before she had gone very far, she turned and shouted: 'I almost forgot! They've dug something up over there!'

'What's that?' asked Olavi.

54

'Áddjá is at his wit's end!'

'What have they dug up?' Olavi repeated to himself. Bigga-Marja stopped bouncing the ball and looked to one side. Something about the girl's movements led him to guess before she let out a sound. Perhaps it was because she seemed slightly on edge, though she tried to hide it with characteristic spirit and by bouncing her ball. But Olavi knew what it was.

'The prison camp,' Bigga shouted frantically in a high, affected tone. 'That's why Áddjá is here, and Matilda the pig.'

The two looked at each other for a moment. Olavi did not reply, and Bigga did not continue. He knew she was waiting for him to say something, but what could he possibly say?

There was nothing to say.

Eventually she turned, ran back down to the worksite, the sunshine sparkling against the side of the cradle-ball, and left Olavi to his own quiet solitude.

INARI

Mar. 1944

TODAY, KALLE, Heiskanen and I cleaned out the tents. This is normally the prisoners' job, but every so often we have to inspect them to make sure there is nothing untoward stowed away, no suspect objects or things of that nature.

I haven't seen these Finnish tents before, though they were advertised in flyers with typical Finnish pride throughout the war. These tent structures are round and tall enough for a man to stand upright. On the floor there is room for twenty or so to sleep next to one another, and more on the bunk beds.

They are surely better than the German tents, and most certainly better than the Soviet ones. You can tell the ramshackle German things just by touching them. They sway somehow differently, and they don't last many winters; some barely survive a single one. As spring arrives, they collapse under the weight of wet packing snow. Word has it that, a few weeks back, around fifty prisoners perished when a tent collapsed in Rovaniemi the morning after some exceptionally heavy snowfall. Perhaps it was already four or five weeks ago. Here at the camp, time is a concept that doesn't really exist. At least, not as we have learnt to understand it. Nonetheless, after the tent structures collapsed, they had to dig the bodies out from under the snow. It is a bothersome task, because you have to make sure your shovel doesn't accidentally slice through any of the skulls.

As we cleaned the tent, I noticed that the plywood slats were covered in carved initials, birthplaces, Nazi symbols and whatever else had come to the prisoners' minds. Someone had written out the word God, then an exclamation mark for each day spent in the camp. Thirty-two in total.

Before we finished, we found the skeleton of a small animal, a bird perhaps, or a lemming, in a pile in the corner. None of us cleared it away.

Mar. 1944

The clear weather is beautiful but biting cold. The prisoners do not have enough clothes. Every morning we find some of them frozen to death. One of the Karelians from across the border died and was thrown in an open pit.

The birds are clearly beginning to sing more. We try to take some extra straw from the horse feed and give it to the birds. Later in the spring, the tits and sparrows might provide more food. When Heiskanen and I were drawing up a list of necessary provisions this morning, he told me that last year he and Kalle had tried to turn the fenced-off area between the barn and the doctor's cabin into a vegetable patch, and that he had asked for permission to do the same this year too. Heiskanen was visibly excited at the idea, and explained that before coming here he used to work in a garden and that was why he knew which vegetables could grow here and which would yield the greatest crop.

As I took the order list to Felde, I saw a prisoner, frozen to death, his body propped against the trunk of one of the low-standing trees. The man was stark naked. Frozen in his arms were a few twigs and branches, his bony fingers clenched around them. He had been left out there as a warning to the others. He hadn't let go of his twigs at any point.

Mar. 1944

I received orders to take some of the prisoners who arrived last week to the doctor's cabin. The waiting room was almost full. One of the men in there was bragging, pointing to the knee of his trousers where there was a white, flaking blotch. A Finnish girl's lusty sap, he laughed, and described pressing his leg into the woman's groin, gently rubbing it against her, and before long she was mewling like a cat in heat, apparently pleading with him to enter her, there behind the house in broad daylight, right in front of everybody. The man boasted that he should cut off a piece of the fabric and keep it under his pillow, so that he could sniff it in the evenings and first thing in the morning. For a small fee, he would let the others sniff it too.

We all laughed. Of course, the damned bloodletter happened into the room at precisely that moment. She only glanced at me in passing, as I gave her the paperwork I had filled out and handed over the prisoners. Her hair was loose, its hairpin missing. I tried to apologize for the coarse language. She said nothing to me, she barely even looked at me. All I saw was the glimmer of electric violet in those eyes.

It was only as I was leaving the doctor's cabin that something dawned on me. When the bloodletter came from the surgery into the waiting room, she had left the door open behind her. In the surgery, the other Karelian prisoner was lying on the trolley, clearly lifeless. I hadn't realized that he too had perished.

Later that night, I awoke to the sound of the body being taken away from the camp. I saw Kalle and Heiskanen loading it on to a truck.

Mar. 1944

The night-time disposal of the body and what I had seen in the doctor's surgery puzzled me. I have been asking around about the bloodletter. Somebody told me she is from Varangerfjord or somewhere even further afield, a relic of a bygone era, descended from the Ainu people or the Congolese negroes. Another prisoner claimed that she wasn't from Varangerfjord at all; apparently, she was a Lapp from Inari or Utsjoki, a Skolt from Petsamo, or she belonged to one of the Finnish tribes in the Kola Peninsula. A third source said she was one of the Kven people from Finnmark. Perhaps she was all of the above, a mongrel. Whatever she was, the general opinion was that she was certainly a degenerate element. 'Is she a prisoner?' I asked, but nobody seemed to know one way or the other. She has been here as long as anybody can remember.

She has been here since the very beginning.

ENONTEKIÖ, 1947

INKERI STOOD in the freezing-cold darkroom and wondered about the house's insulation. She slid a large sheet of paper into the basin of developing fluid, checking to make sure the paper became completely immersed first time. Then she took a clothes peg from beside her, pressed the paper beneath the surface of the liquid and began gently rocking the basin back and forth, mentally counting the seconds. This was the most critical phase of the process. For a moment longer, she rinsed the image in developing fluid, which she had mixed herself from the materials that were available. In the past she had even used coffee.

Inkeri had taken very ordinary shots of the areas where she had wandered. Nothing special, only landscapes, she assured herself. Throughout the summer and autumn months she had asked the locals—usually those whom she had interviewed for a story—whether they knew anything about the events that had taken place here during the war, places where there might have been soldiers, camps, anything at all. Prisoners, even. Whenever someone had shown her a possible site, she had photographed it in the hope that the images might reveal something to her. But they never did.

Using the clothes peg, Inkeri lifted the paper out of the dark fluid. There it was—the negative of a landscape with a fell rising up in the background and where, according to someone she had spoken to, there had once been a tent or barracks of some description. Inkeri quickly transferred the paper to the next basin. The function of this second phase was to stop the development begun by the first. Inkeri caught the powerful smell of chemicals and licked her lips. She thought she could see small bubbles at the edge of the basin. That was the acid working. A moment later she picked up the clothes peg again, removed the paper, dipped it into the basin of fixer and gave a sigh. Without even noticing, she had been holding her breath. Sometimes, preparing a photograph felt like a sprint. Last of all, she placed the image into a bowl of water and gave it a shake. The water radiated with cold. Her fingers felt numb. Then she hung the photograph on the clothes line alongside the others to dry.

She switched on the lights.

Inkeri rubbed her fingers and blew on them. That constant, sweet chill. The pain. She glanced at her watch. She was in a hurry to get to work.

She took her satchel from the hallway and dashed into the frigid air outside. The frost had formed pearls around the door-frame. Autumn had been a blaze of handsome, resplendent colour, and now the only memory of that crimson glow was the leaves lying dead on the path. Inkeri had begun her art classes a month ago. When she said she wanted to teach the children art, the headmaster had laughed at her request and treated it like the whim of a small child. He said he would agree if Inkeri could provide the pupils with all necessary equipment; the school could not afford such things. Two weeks later, Inkeri had returned to the school and shown the headmaster a list of all the equipment she had managed to source through her own contacts. 'Watercolours? For everyone?' said the headmaster in astonishment. Watercolours, charcoals, paper. Everything they could possibly imagine.

Inkeri's class was not really a lesson in the traditional sense. It was an extra-curricular activity held after school, but many of the children took part. At the first lesson, the classroom was full of people, both pupils and staff, the latter attending more out of curiosity than anything else. Now most of them had disappeared. Inkeri had begun the first lesson by asking something she thought would bring the Sámi and the Finnish children together. 'Now, let's begin with you telling me the Sámi word for the arts!' The pupils were sitting at their desks in front of her. Those who didn't have a desk of their own sat on the floor.

'We don't have a word for that,' someone muttered after a short silence. The response made some of the Finnish children giggle. One of the Sámi pupils scowled at them and stuck out her tongue.

'The arts? There's really no word for it?' Inkeri asked them. She was incredulous: for centuries, the arts had been the hallmark of civilized cultures, and the people up here didn't even have a word for the concept. How far she was from the world she knew. Her manner of approaching the pupils had fallen flat. Eventually, Bigga-Marja raised her hand.

'*Dáidu* might work.'

'Good. What does that mean?'

'Skill. Understanding.'

'Perfect! Because that's exactly what art *is*! It's about skill and understanding,' Inkeri had commented, relieved, and continued with the class. But every time she walked to the school, she remembered that moment, that unsettling feeling that had engulfed her. She was very far away from everything familiar. If Kenya had felt like the edge of the earth, this place was further still.

Inkeri opened the door into her classroom, which was already full of children. They had taken out their painting equipment and were continuing from where they had left off last time. Inkeri had given them permission to start without her.

'Hello, everyone, nice to see you all getting stuck in,' she said, shrugging off her coat. There was an argument going on in one corner of the room, and Inkeri looked up to see what was happening. One of the boys had daubed another boy's face with watercolours.

'Right, silence!' she shouted, and clapped her hands. The children immediately stopped what they were doing and sat down at their desks. Inkeri did not continue speaking until there was perfect silence in the room. 'Today we are going to talk about colour values,' she said in a stern voice, then she took out a piece of chalk and began drawing patterns on the green board. She drew a circle upon which she began marking pairs of colours.

'Colours—what wonderful things they are! Their qualities and characters are constantly changing, just like people's. They can be cold, pure, broken or warm, and their brightness and darkness, that is, their colour value, can change. For instance, yellow is a bright, brilliant colour, but its complementary colour, violet, is not,' she explained, then began asking the pupils about complementary colours and writing them on the board. How do colours behave when they are next to another colour? What does indigo look like next to a cold yellow? Or how about when it is next to ultramarine? Everything is linked to the background, and things can look quite different when seen out of context.

Inkeri noticed she had started explaining relatively new research: the construction of colours, light waves, the fact that invisible rays were running before our very eyes. It wasn't until she mentioned Albert Einstein that she realized she had drifted off into a complicated lecture. She turned to the class and asked, now somewhat amused:

'Do you have the slightest idea what I'm talking about?'

The pupils laughed and shook their heads. Inkeri smiled and put down the stick of chalk.

'I'm sorry. I was just developing some photographs at home. And whenever I develop them, I find myself going into something of a… a *trance*,' she explained. 'I become so caught up in what I'm doing that I can't even see in front of me.' The pupils laughed again.

'Very well. Now, use your watercolours to paint something using complementary colours. I'll give you an example,' she said, and took an object from her pocket.

'This is a genuine lion's furball.' Inkeri had been carrying it with her for years, right from the outbreak of the war, in fact. 'I will hand it around the class. And your task is to paint me a lion using complementary colours and everything we have just learnt.'

Just as she had guessed, the lion's furball was a source of great excitement. The children couldn't wait for their turn to touch it, running over to admire it as it made its way around the classroom. Inkeri watched them contentedly. The pupils could hardly imagine how rare the object really was. Hair from a white lion. At first, Inkeri had thought the white lion was an imaginary creature, the stuff of myths and fairy tales like the unicorn. All across Africa, people told stories about sighting this great animal. But it really did exist after all. Inkeri would never forget the day when she laid eyes on the creature for the first time. Back then, when her marriage to Kaarlo was all but over, besides taking up a raft of lovers, Inkeri had found a new hobby: hunting. Of course, it wasn't the first time she had ventured out into the forests, but in the past she had stayed back and watched as the men raised their weapons and quaffed gin and tonics while the women clapped demurely at their achievements.

On her first hunting trip, Inkeri had taken with her a group of workers from the plantation. The local tribesmen were to serve as her security and vowed to protect her on pain of death, but they also provided her with some much-needed company. Everything had been planned for months, and she opted to make the trip once the rainy season had come to an end. The great plains of the savannah were awash with floodwaters. The incessant humidity made it feel like being in a sauna. The trip lasted a week in total, and by the end of the second day they had already killed a couple of antelopes and a rhinoceros whose hide Inkeri eventually had made into a table. On the penultimate evening, they ate giraffe steaks as the gramophone spilt music across the plains.

'Is it really a lion's furball?' one of the children asked all of a sudden. Inkeri woke from her reverie.

'Yes, it is.'

'I thought lions were yellow. This is white.'

'That's why it is so rare,' said Inkeri with a smile.

'It's a bit like a white reindeer's fur, but smoother!' someone shouted.

A little boy dressed in a Sámi cap and costume whispered something to the fair-haired boy next to him, and a moment later the fair boy raised his hand.

'Yes?'

'Ántte here wants to know if there are any reindeer in Kenya,' asked Niila.

'Next time, Ántte can ask me all by himself—in clear Finnish, just like everybody else. No, there are no reindeer in Kenya. But there are pigs,' said Inkeri, watching as Bigga-Marja raised the furball up to the light. Until now, the girl hadn't paid it much attention. Instead, she had been eagerly writing down Inkeri's answers in her jotter.

After the first few lessons, Bigga-Marja had appeared at Inkeri's desk and asked her: 'What is light?' Inkeri placed her pencil on the table and wondered whether the girl was making fun of her or whether she really did want to know. She wanted to know lots of things. What does light mean? What is photography? What is darkness? How do you transfer the image on to the paper? Is light alive? What are colours made of, if you can't see them without light; and so on and so forth. Inkeri answered these questions in a cool, somewhat offhand manner. Bigga listened to her without saying a word, then she shrugged her shoulders and walked away, and she never mentioned the subject again.

Inkeri watched as Bigga-Marja passed the furball to the next pupil, then returned to her memories. The final morning of their first hunting expedition broke to a thick mist, and as the mist gradually dispersed a herd of a thousand buffaloes slowly came into view. And at that very moment she saw it, gleaming in the morning sunshine: a white lioness. The animal was alone, was stalking the buffaloes, and she must have been ravenous to attack a herd that size. The thousand-strong herd was the most dangerous thing she would ever encounter in the savannah. Tense and hidden, Inkeri watched the great cat's attack and the ensuing struggle. She looked on as the lioness tore her prey to shreds, ate it all alone, and began dragging the carcass to the east once she had taken her fill. Inkeri named her Alba, the white one.

Back in the classroom, Inkeri caught a conversation between Niila and one of the Finnish children. 'Have you heard what the builders found down at the church?' Niila asked the other boy.

'I heard my father talking about it! And I heard that the Kolehmainen boys have already been down there hunting for treasure. I wonder if there's anything left to find.'

'Shall we go there this evening and look?' asked Niila.

'I don't know, there might still be mines in the ground...'

Something about their conversation made Inkeri walk up to them. Niila had already painted a yellow lion against a violet background.

'What are you boys plotting?'

The boys looked at each other, startled, then shrugged their shoulders.

'Haven't you heard, Miss?'

'Heard about what?'

Niila watched her, then turned to look at another, slightly shorter boy.

'The prison camp—or what's left of it. They've dug it up, right next to the new church,' the boy mumbled, and when he saw Inkeri's expression he continued. 'Right opposite this school.' Inkeri was engulfed with a sharp chill, as though a cold, scaly hand had pushed its way inside her and was now tugging at her heart and the pit of her stomach. She felt sick.

'A prison camp? Right opposite the school…?' she asked, and the boys nodded. She suddenly caught Bigga-Marja's eye. The girl was staring right at her, and there was something about her expression that Inkeri couldn't make out. Bigga looked away, leaving only a dim, flat emptiness.

INARI

Mar. 1944

ELDE ASKED to see me for the first time since my arrival. We went through a few formalities. For some reason, he wanted to know who my supervisor was during my time at Stalag 309. The question took me by surprise. I hadn't given any thought to Tapani Koskela for a long time. What's more, on his desk I saw that Felde had German translations of all my documents, including my membership of the Patriotic People's Movement and the Academic Karelia Society. I don't know how he acquired them. I certainly hadn't sent them. At least, I don't remember sending them.

Before leaving, I asked him what had happened to the Finnish prisoners. If they are not moved to the Finnish camps, will they receive instruction here? Surely one of the women from the Lotta Brigade must be able to teach them language and religion. According to Felde, the Lotta whores were only good for one thing. Slightly hesitating, I asked whether the bodies of the Finnish prisoners were taken somewhere else. The grandfather clock struck the hour, punctuating the silence.

'Do you know why Hänninen was moved to other duties?' the commander asked me, a chilling note in his voice. I didn't know. He explained that Hänninen had started to become a security risk. 'He asked too many questions too.'

I lowered my eyes.

'What is your opinion of Private Heiskanen?' he then enquired.

'I don't have an opinion of him,' I replied. 'He seems friendly with the Finnish prisoner.'

'Indeed. Heiskanen feels a certain sympathy towards the weaker races. From there, it is only a short leap to race betrayal. Furthermore, it has come to my attention that the Finnish Security Police are surprisingly well informed about what goes on at these camps. They even had an agent here once. I am quite certain that Hänninen was the informant. But I can't be sure. One cannot be sure of anything. I don't know whether I can trust you, either.'

'Of course you can, Commander, sir,' I hurried to assure him. Instinctively, I glanced over at the Order of the Day, framed and hanging on the wall. I did not spend time reading it again. I didn't have to; I can still remember von Falkenhorst's words almost verbatim: *In defence of Finland's security and European culture, we shall take up arms against the arch-enemy, as our fathers did before us in 1918.*

'If you notice anything out of the ordinary about Heiskanen, sending any extra letters, perhaps, then you will tell me. If he's a traitor, or even an agent passing information to the FSP, we will have to get rid of him,' said Felde with a note of irritation.

I told him what I had seen the previous evening. Felde shrugged his shoulders, smacked his lips.

'That is a special operation… You don't need to know anything about it, at least not yet…' he said with a wave of the hand.

As I left, my gaze fell upon the photograph frames on Felde's desk. I don't know what they show, but I can imagine them containing pictures of people posing for the camera. Perhaps they no longer contain anything at all.

Mar. 1944

It has been calm and quiet here, quite boring in fact. The only excitement is that the reindeer have been found dead near the camp with greater regularity than before. In the past they merely used to set off the alarms, and they can cause considerable damage if they step on a mine. Kalle and a few other prisoners have been assigned to drag the carcasses away, using a metal detector to keep themselves safe. But Kalle remained with the guards on this side of the mine fence. Kalle, the other guards and I all stand further off and wait for one of the prisoners to step on a mine, privately hoping they die instantly. Listening to the sounds of a man dying in agony is excruciating. If that happens, all we can do is take aim and put the poor soul out of his misery. From this distance, you might have to shoot several times before hitting the target.

The increase in reindeer deaths is a pity. There is already a lack of reindeer, and there aren't enough fattened animals to be slaughtered for food. The state and the Nazis have forcibly expropriated most of the herding cooperatives' reindeer, which is presumably one reason why relations between the Nazis and the local communities here have begun to fray. On top of this, I heard that the regiment has been waiting for weeks for new consignments of reindeer to replace those that have been killed. Once they have been checked for disease, at least dead reindeer still provide meat.

Mar. 1944

Because things have been so tedious, I spent the evening helping the bloodletter enter prisoner details in the ledger. She does all kinds of jobs around here. There is a shortage of doctors, and we know that she can do all manner of things. A small, dappled spitz was scuttling around the room with her. Like a Finnish Spitz, but not quite. It is one of the permanent dogs at the camp, but, unlike the others, this dog isn't used for guarding duties or to locate any runaway prisoners. This dog is for hunting.

I asked the bloodletter what her name was. She glared at me and showed me her green residence card, though I hadn't asked to see it. 'Can't trust you Nazis with a thing like this,' she said, looking me right in the eye. I swear that in a certain light her eyes are almost violet. 'I am not a Nazi,' I stammered. I don't know why I said that. Why was I suddenly so embarrassed? I have nothing to be ashamed of. The bloodletter laughed and didn't avert her eyes. Again, I asked her name.

'It says here, in plain Finnish: Saara,' she said impassively, took out her silver lighter and lit a cigarette. 'Saara Valva.'

'Väinö Remes,' I introduced myself, and held out my hand. Saara put the cigarette between her lips, her eyes still fixed upon me, took a long drag on it, sucking her cheeks in, then

folded her arms and raised her chin, seemingly with no intention of taking my hand. 'Väinö Remes,' she said, her voice
low, slowly elongating each vowel as though mentioning the
name of a particularly unpleasant dish, a squid or a jellyfish.
Eventually she placed a pile of papers in my outstretched hand
and instructed me to write down what she dictated. Naturally,
I did not say no.

She didn't once look at me again all evening, but there we
were, the two of us, breathing in the same air. At one point
she accidentally touched my jacket sleeve, and now I cannot
think of anything else.

Mar. 1944

In a few days' time, we will be heading off to begin the construction of a new road to the Törmänen airfield. We can choose
which prisoners to take with us. We will take the ones in best
physical condition and also a few weaker ones, simply to be
able to bury them elsewhere.

Heiskanen is coming too.

Mar. 1944

I find it strange that Felde didn't ask me to pay attention to
Kalle's movements. But I have been watching him all the same.
I have come to the conclusion that Kalle is a secret inform-
ant, a prisoner who has been tasked with spying on the other

prisoners. Thus far, I have seen people like this at every camp I have visited. Either that, or something else entirely is afoot. And as I think this, I realize that even if Kalle is a secret informant, something else entirely probably is afoot.

Mar. 1944

Tomorrow night the theatre group will present their new work. They are going to perform a play written by one of the prisoners who claims to be a playwright. Who knows? Around here, anyone can concoct themselves a different past. Some of the prisoners are constantly fabricating a fresh web of stories about themselves that they tell the new prisoners. One week they are heirs to the throne, another they are famous writers. It is entertaining to watch.

I like the theatre group. Some of the members are actually very skilful actors. One of the prisoners interprets everything from Russian into German. The leading actor has changed again. The man suspected of being a Jew was sent to another camp about twenty kilometres to the north, where the Germans keep the Jewish prisoners. Another of the actors was executed the day before yesterday, and the whole play has been put together again from scratch.

We rehearse near the lake, at the point where the under-current means the water never freezes. This is where we get our drinking water. Out here, the prisoners speak more freely. At one point, I suddenly realized they were talking about the nocturnal transportations. I asked what they knew about them.

They looked at one another, startled, now unable to take the words back. I asked again, and at the same time wondered if they might know whether the dead were transported somewhere too.

They nodded, said that sometimes dead prisoners were even dug up from their graves.

'Who makes the decision?' I queried.

'It depends, but lately it has been the bloodletter. Sometimes the doctor,' one of the women said timidly. 'They know best about the condition and race of the bodies.'

Mar. 1944

Today was the final rehearsal with the theatre group, and the performance will be later this evening. We were just about to finish when one of the prisoners gave a shout. I turned to see what all the fuss was, my weapon at the ready, but it was only a grey swan. It was already big, likely from last year's brood. It was alone and shy. It popped its head from behind a birch tree, and we wondered why the swan was still here and, more to the point, how it was still alive. It must have been crippled, broken-winged or otherwise injured. The animal approached us cautiously, its head bobbing jerkily. It let out a small cry that didn't sound like a swan, or any other creature for that matter. We had food with us, and the prisoners gave the swan some crumbs. The creature was in need of affection; it came up very close. The prisoners stroked its body and patted its head. Pristine white feathers were already poking their way through the bird's coat. It didn't have a mother. She must have died in the war or flown away before the onset of winter, leaving her cygnet behind.

The swan's eyes were gleaming, meek.

When I shot it, the creature's gaze remained fixed on the sky, on a small white cloud slowly gliding past.

ENONTEKIÖ, 1947

O F ALL THE REALMS of consciousness we know, dreams are the most curious. In ancient times, people used to believe that we could give away half of our heart and soul and that those given-away halves wandered in the spirit world, in our dreams. When he woke up, Olavi gasped for breath, filled his lungs with oxygen, as though he had just swum to the surface of the water. He focused on the ceiling and tried to calm down, counted to ten, eleven, fifteen, twenty-five. The attic room had a low ceiling, a lattice of different beams and timbers. Sharp nails protruded from one of them, and when Olavi looked at them he thought of birth and death and what might lie between them. Was it worth anything?

The temperature had plummeted overnight; he had felt it in the creaking of the beams. By the time he emptied the chamber pot out of the window, a skim of ice had formed across the surface of the urine. The acrid smell caught in his nostrils. As he closed the window, he saw that the frost flowers on the windowpane were beginning to melt. He had placed a small mountain plant in a pot on the windowsill. He kept it there so that it could catch what little light there was. He gave it just enough water to struggle on a while longer, but not enough for it to push out a flower. A faint light filtered in through the window. Broken branches battered against the pane, scraping and grating back and forth across the glass. Apart from that, everything was quiet. Olavi noticed a tiny snowflake melting against the windowpane. It slid slowly down the glass and eventually disappeared altogether.

The workers at the construction site had been instructed not to talk about what had been discovered, especially not to outsiders and particularly not to reporters. The word 'reporter' could only refer to Inkeri. In public, it was to be described as a minefield, detritus from the war, that sort of thing. Officially, the matter was to be passed on to the authorities, but the workers hadn't done this. Then the inevitable happened.

The boys from Kolehmainen's shop, the youngest of whom was only seven, had found what was left of the camp. Naturally, they had tried to sell things they found there to travelling smugglers. The second time they went to rummage through the debris, they took more people with them. The youngest of the boys stepped on a mine and died on the spot. After this the area with the mines was cordoned off, and the matter was turned over to the police in no time. For this reason, the site might remain off-limits for weeks, and this in turn affected the construction of the church.

Olavi sighed. He washed his face and groin, relieved himself into the chamber pot, and inspected between his toes, a habit he had picked up during the war, then pulled on his clothes and walked downstairs into the quiet kitchen. He ate, made some coffee, drank the coffee. He sat on the kitchen bench and listened to the silence. Inkeri wasn't at home. She had left early that morning on a photography excursion. That suited him fine. He didn't know how to be in the same room as her. She put him on edge; they so rarely had anything to say to each other.

As he left, Olavi closed the latch on the door, walked past the well and the dead tree. It was dark, the ground frozen hard beneath his feet. As he arrived at the construction site, it was clear that work hadn't progressed today either. He walked past a group of unfamiliar men in suits and ties, each with a fur hat on his head. He did not greet them but instead strode right up to the church without turning his head. Men like that were here almost every day, investigating minerals, investigating the soil. Investigating people too. Piera was sitting quietly, waiting for him. He had started working at the construction site as well; it seems the old man didn't know what to do with himself otherwise. He was drinking coffee that gave off a cheap, pungent smell. A small cloud of steam rose from his burl mug and mixed with the smoke from Olavi's cigarette, and for a moment the two men couldn't be told apart. There was only around an hour of daylight left, if that. The darkness felt safe.

'Morning,' said Piera, his eyes fixed on the men in suits. Olavi did not respond. 'Men like that are five a penny. Come up here, sticking their noses in, taking away minerals and what have you, and they talk all funny and southern so you can't understand a word,' Piera muttered, and spat on the ground.

Olavi looked at the men. 'They here because of the camp?' he asked, instinctively slipping his hand into his pocket to fumble for a cigarette, though he didn't really want one. It was a force of habit.

'Doubt it. At least, I don't think so. They look too perky and greedy. Must be some other reason. Besides, none of 'em knows there's a camp here in the first place.'

'Even if they did, nobody'd be interested,' Olavi remarked.

'Right,' he scoffed, and threw a pebble to the ground. 'Seems this church is going to be another one for the Laplanders and all. Bigga-Marja told me they spent a week in a church during the evacuation, because there was nowhere else to go. Said it was cold in there. Some of 'em came down with pneumonia. And died.'

'Churches are like that,' said Olavi. Piera began digging some tobacco from his pocket and stuffing the strands into his pipe.

'Sometimes I wonder, would it have made any difference if I'd gone with her? Or if they'd stayed on the Finnish side, gone to Ostrobothnia or somewhere like that? But you can't sing hymns in Sámi in Finnish churches neither. And I know for a fact it'll be forbidden in this church too. One word of Sámi is one too many.'

Olavi crouched down to pick up a spade from the ground.

'Hah, leave it be, lad,' Piera snapped, and Olavi dropped the spade without any questions.

Once again Piera had brought along his little grunting friend, which gleefully scampered between the two men in the hope of some attention. He had put a collar with a small bell on the pig. Olavi scratched beneath the collar, and the creature's left hind trotter began rhythmically pawing the ground.

'Her coat's thicker,' said Olavi, the cigarette hanging from the corner of his mouth.

'Oh, yes. Isn't that right, Matilda? *Oh, yes*,' Piera babbled to the pig. Olavi patted Matilda's soft snout. The pig was stunted, smaller than the other pigs from the litter. *Some damned genetic defect*, Piera often commented, but this did nothing to dampen the pig's mirth. Olavi took a sip of coffee without a word. Further off, someone had lit a bonfire at the spot where the workers usually had their break. The rest of the labourers were down there. The sun was finally peeping from between the clouds. Olavi and Piera joined the others.

'Did you hear one of the Kolehmainen boys managed to find an old car tyre and other wartime junk down there and sold it to the smugglers? He got himself caught, mind, and now he's doing time in the county jail while the law decides what to do with him. He's only twelve, but sure he'll end up at a work camp, you mark my words,' a voice boomed. Olavi listened in as the men began discussing the fate of the Kolehmainen family. Piera had struck up another conversation and was telling one of the Quakers about the war in his own quirky English.

Olavi smiled. He had found Piera quite puzzling at first—a man who knew so many languages. He had learnt English in correspondence with his cousin, all because of a newspaper advertisement in the late nineteenth century inviting Sámi people to move to Alaska and teach the locals the art of reindeer-herding. Legend had it that the newcomers had shot all the native peoples to the brink of extinction, only to realize they didn't know how to build a livelihood in the harsh northern conditions and needed those who did. And so, at the age of fifteen, Piera's uncle set off for the new world. Within ten years he had started a family, and Piera got to know his cousin by post. In many ways, every letter from across the ocean was more valuable than gold. Piera had kept the letters and eventually he began collecting the stamps that adorned their envelopes, stamps from around the world. It seems his cousin eventually joined the circus and travelled all over the United States. At first Piera had thought he must be some kind of magician or a trapeze artist, but it turned out that all his cousin had to do was stand stock still in his Sámi costume with representatives from other native peoples to be gawped at by all and sundry.

Olavi didn't join the conversation but listened as the Quaker explained that he had been a pilot in Italy during the war. Apparently, he had accidentally bombed the Vatican. Well, almost. Olavi heard the two men laughing, and he chuckled too. The Quaker's tall tales were often such great stories that people rarely questioned the veracity of the details. His story-telling brought levity to their workdays, and that's why people liked the man. It was the same during the war too. The best storyteller was often more use than the most accurate sniper.

Olavi let the pig go on her way, having been petting her absent-mindedly with his free hand. When he turned his head, he noticed a figure in the distance walking right towards them. It was curious the way one could identify a person this far away, without hearing their voice, just from the contours of their movements.

'Too old to go to war, me. I stayed here, took care of things,' he heard Piera explaining when the Quaker asked to hear his stories about the war.

'What about you?' the Quaker asked, and pointed at Olavi.

Olavi said nothing. He stood up, lit a cigarette, looked at the figure approaching. Piera chatted with the Quaker a while longer, then he too stood up and walked over to Olavi. Just then, Inkeri reached them and stopped to listen to the men's conversation. She squinted and examined the pig but said nothing. Only then did she look up and notice Olavi. He raised his hand by way of a greeting. Eventually, everyone else fell silent too.

'Come and join us under the tarp, lass! We won't bite!' one of the labourers shouted, and added a crude joke for good measure. The men chortled, all except Olavi and Piera. Inkeri didn't seem to pay them any attention; instead she gazed around unperturbed, as though she was looking for something in particular. Then she turned to Olavi. They stared at each other for a long moment. It seemed as though something was bothering her. Olavi didn't know what to say, and Inkeri said nothing either. She tucked a pale curl of hair behind her ear and held the camera safe beneath her coat. The coat looked heavy, but it was clearly still damp from the recent snowfall. Her lips were slightly open, and she looked as though she was on the verge of saying something, but nothing came out; then, just as suddenly as she had arrived, she turned without saying a word.

Olavi sat down and watched as she walked away.

'Is it true that old maid used to be a correspondent in Africa?' asked the labourer, having now lost face, and it took a moment before Olavi realized that the question was addressed to him.

'Apparently so.'

'With her husband?'

Olavi didn't reply.

'I heard her husband was a shareholder in a tobacco company. Or owned one himself,' someone commented on Olavi's behalf.

'It's a queer thing when a grown woman goes gallivanting around the wilds with a contraption like that. Like folk you see wandering around without a clue where they're going. Running, more like it!'

'She's a widow, isn't she? I heard her man disappeared in the war,' someone snapped, and with that the conversation calmed down and soon moved on to another topic. Piera sat down and beckoned to Olavi.

'Listen up,' said Piera, almost under his breath, making sure nobody else was within earshot.

'What?'

'A little bird tells me your landlady's been going around asking the villagers things that don't tally up with her story about being a reporter and that.'

'A little bird, eh? And what kind of bird was that?'

'A smart one. One that can put two and two together. Inkeri's digging around in what happened during the war. Asking about the camps too, she is.'

Olavi was suddenly alert and frowned. 'She hasn't asked me.'

'You didn't tell her that's what's left of the old camp?'

'Of course not!'

'Well, Bigga said one of the other pupils mentioned it, and Inkeri turned white as a sheet. There's something not quite right about that lass.'

'What do you mean?' Olavi asked. Now he too had lowered his voice.

Matilda suddenly appeared at Olavi's feet. He stroked her sheep-like coat. Pigs made good test animals. Their bodies were very like human bodies. And they were intelligent beings. German animal tests had shown that a pig can die within a week from sleep deprivation. Humans didn't last much longer.

Towards the end, humans experienced hallucinations, their speech became incomprehensible and their eyes already looked dead. The body temperature dropped and the organs almost went into hibernation to conserve energy. A foetid stench came from the mouth, and no matter how much you washed, the skin felt dirty. It began to flake and peel off. *Weakened state of awareness*; that's what was written on the subject's medical card. It was a gruesome sight. The dying patient might still last days, weeks, but by that point there was nothing that could be done.

'It's strange, 'cause it makes you wonder why she's come here in the first place. One thing's for sure: it's not just so she can write articles for the paper about dwarf reindeer that don't even exist,' Piera hissed.

Olavi scratched the hair beneath his cap and swallowed. A small, dark blotch had begun to spread through his body, and that told him Piera was right.

'Well, she's hiding something all right. You mark my words.'

INARI

Mar. 1944

W E HAVE BEEN in the middle of nowhere for a week now. We finally set off to build the road to the airfield. The prisoners do the work, and we oversee them. During this time, I have learnt that the Luftwaffe airfield at Törmänen is a coveted workplace. The prisoners are only too keen to be sent there. You can sometimes find useful things on the aeroplanes, especially in among any wreckage. Clothes, even food. If the guard is amenable, he will let you keep it too.

Today we saw at least five planes land and take off.

Mar. 1944

The days are getting longer. The change seems to happen all at once. At first the difference is subtle, only twenty minutes or so, then in the space of only a few days the amount of light seems to have increased immeasurably. Before long, day will be longer than night.

I am lying in the shelter and admiring the sky. I watch an aeroplane taking off. The sunlight strikes its wing. Then it disappears into a cloud and I cannot see it any more.

When I close my eyes, I catch the fragrance of spring in the air.

Mar. 1944

There is not much to do here, so I have to listen to Heiskanen rattling on. He's certainly no priest—he is a horticulturalist! I have not heard him say a single word about God, though he talks incessantly about flowers.

Here in the north there is a very special low-lying undergrowth across the fells, the type one does not encounter anywhere else in Finland, or in Europe for that matter, with the possible exception of the Alps. The flowers blossom low to the ground, forming a beautiful mattress across the terrain where you can lie down and sleep. Heiskanen tells me that, standing at the top of the fell on a clear day, you can stare out across the landscape, a hundred kilometres from one side of the horizon to the other, a soft sea of wild flora as far as the eye can see. I don't believe I have ever known anything like it, not even during my time across the border. Besides, back then we were much further to the south.

Mar. 1944

We spent the evening playing chess. The prisoners are housed in barracks dotted here and there and guarded by the camp's Lapphunds. Kalle sleeps in our quarters. Heiskanen has with him a small wooden folding chessboard, so the evenings pass quickly, otherwise it would be deathly boring here. Kalle sometimes plays with us too.

The bright weather has brought with it biting temperatures. But it is beautiful. Today we were able to go flying. Seen from the air in calm weather, the road workers and their camps look like a rosary of pearls.

Mar. 1944

Commander Felde gave me a copy of Svinhufvud's new book, *A Testament to My People*. He received this copy from Hitler himself. I have been leafing through it in the evenings. Heiskanen wondered what I was reading. I showed him the book and asked if he had read it. He said he has no intentions of ever reading another book published by the SS. I chuckled and asked whether he had already had enough after reading the *Prisoner-of-War Interrogation Guide*. During my training this was the only book we ever used. He laughed and nodded. We chatted for a while longer. Before going to sleep, I read the following passage: '... the struggle towards this end is yet unfinished, but this struggle shall continue with unflinching resolve and power until victory is ours. And when it is time to assess the achievements of this war, our contribution to the battle will surely be found of merit, for our goal, the creation of a Greater Finland, shall not be considered an excess, but a matter of the utmost justice and righteousness.'

Mar. 1944

The prisoners are carrying out repair work, erecting fences and ploughing the roads. An order has been given to cut down all remaining trees. There is still a little strip of forest at Törmänen, but once that has been cleared the only woodland left will be on a small island near Kasariselkä in Lake Inari, where we will go once the ice has melted. We don't quite know what to do; there are no more trees to chop down. The poles for the snow fences and supporting beams will require hundreds of metres of wood.

Mar. 1944

The road connection between Inari, Kaamanen and Karigasniemi is nearly finished, while in western Lapland work on the road from Palojoensuu to Skibotn and from there further north has commenced in good time. These roads are intended to reach all the way to the Arctic Ocean. The road between Ivalo and Inari has been widened for a stretch of almost thirty kilometres. Bridges are under construction too, and these will eventually replace boat connections. Everything that can be extracted here is quite rightly being sent to Germany. Soon the whole Petsamo region will have been mined of all its nickel. Some time ago, Organization Todt transferred some of our prisoners to the hydroelectric plant at Jäniskoski. The intention was to build a protective dome over the plant so that neither the Soviets nor the Allies would be able to blow it up and disrupt power production. Before coming here, Heiskanen used to work on the Hyrynsalmi–Kuusamo route and said that this too was due to be extended east to Kiestinki.

Heiskanen beat me at chess again today, but Kalle beat him three times. In the past we used to reward Kalle's victories by giving him an extra potato, but now we cannot give even that. The spud prize, we laughed. Kalle carried it around with him for days. I'm unsure whether he has eaten it yet.

Mar. 1944

One of the Finnish-speaking prisoners from across the border died yesterday. But he will not be buried. Heiskanen is determined that the body be taken back to the camp. When I tried to ask him the reason why, he wouldn't look at me. When I asked again, he turned towards me and said: 'Why don't you ask Commander Felde?'

Mar. 1944

The trees are all gone.

We have been summoned back to the camp.

ENONTEKIÖ, 1948

IT WAS SLEETING, and Inkeri's steps felt heavy. She gripped the camera in her arms as though she were afraid it might freeze or break. For weeks, she had almost begged Piera to take her to the remains of the prison camp, but he had resolutely refused. There was always an excuse, be it Christmas or New Year or the amount of snow. Inkeri didn't really need Piera's assistance, but entering the area was forbidden and, because of possible mines, walking around could be dangerous.

What is it you're looking for up there? he snapped at her around Christmas time. But after New Year, when she had threatened to go to the area by herself—without a mine detector—Piera finally gave in.

Inkeri looked at the heavy, wet snow around her feet and listened helplessly to the beeping of Piera's metal detector. She nervously puffed on a cigarette, hoping something would happen soon. But, of course, nothing happened. At the same second as she noticed they were making progress, she realized that everything was an illusion. Nothing ever changed, there were always new obstacles in her way, new problems. Snowflakes fell from the tree branches and landed on her boots. She shook the snow loose and cursed.

'Is it safe to come in yet?' she asked, exasperated. Piera

looked back at her and shook his head. Inkeri felt cold. The temperature had started to drop again. Matilda the pig had done her best to sniff out the most important items buried there, whatever they might be. There might have been some decomposing skeletons that could still spread disease, she thought to herself. She glanced at the pig out of the corner of her eye. Piera caught her.

'She's got a *genetic defect*, that's why she's so small,' he noted. Inkeri glared at him and pulled her coat tighter. She took another cigarette out of her pocket and lit it, her hands faintly trembling. The damp seemed to have soaked through her bones and right to the marrow. A small bird flew overhead, let out a weak song.

'They've lost their minds,' said Piera. 'The birds, I mean.'

'Indeed,' Inkeri sighed impatiently. She thought of these dreary grey birds and recalled that in the savannah you could see the most exquisite winged creatures. There were colourful African rollers and kingfishers, peacocks flew here and there, and one could make magnificent fans from their feathers. The peacock's crown, the long black tail feathers of the sakabula.

At first, Inkeri had gone hunting merely for the sport, but sometimes she was able to sell her bounty for money. For the most part, however, all she accrued was honour and reputation. The more stuffed wild beasts that adorned the rooms of their colonial house, the more enchanted the guests became. Using the services of local seamen, she and Kaarlo sent reptiles preserved in glass jars to the zoological museum in Helsinki, stuffed birds and animals, feathers and elephant tusks. The servants usually took care of stuffing the animals, but Inkeri had learnt how to do it herself. Rare birds needed to be stuffed with the utmost care. The creature was first opened up with an incision, either horizontally across the stomach or vertically from the rectum. Then the organs were taken out. The brain had to be removed with a special prong and the eyes dug out with an implement that resembled a small spoon. How many small orifices had Inkeri stared into in the course of her life? That being said, how similar it was looking into a camera without the lens.

'Don't the birds die in all this cold and darkness? Shouldn't they have flown away by now?' she asked.

'So you'd think. But no. Lost their minds, I tell you. Before the war, it was the lemmings that lost their minds. That's how we knew a war was coming.' Piera spoke above the sound of the machine. 'I wonder what it means.'

'Does it have to mean anything?'

'It must mean something.'

'Maybe it means we're going to have good dairy cattle this year.'

'I see… When it's this dark, the heifers' udders don't pro-duce much milk at all. Not even whey,' Piera muttered. Inkeri suddenly caught the smell of wood, sap, sawdust and something stale. She instinctively thought of the stench of rotting corpses and felt a bitter taste in her mouth. She gripped the camera in her arms. Her precious camera. It was the only thing she could really trust.

'And your southern cows don't know how to behave up here neither, they just stand there with their tails drooping and let the midges have their way with them.' The pig moved around impatiently.

'Surely development is a good thing,' she said wearily.

'Now there you're right. You know what I really like, lass?'

'Well?'

'I really like being able to flick a switch and make the lights come on.' Piera winked at her.

'Is that so?' Inkeri mumbled. Piera switched off his machine and looked at her pensively.

'I hear you're writing a newspaper piece about the plans for the reservoir and things like that. Just so it isn't all one-sided, the way things are usually reported in the national news, let me give you my tuppence worth: the south prospers while the north withers. Right this minute, the salmon in Kemi River are dying out. The lakes are filthy. Reindeer wander over on to the wrong side of the border. Soon there'll be no forest left, no fish, no reindeer. For the southerners, it doesn't matter what we live on up here. That's just the way it is, and don't you dare argue back. Let me say my piece,' Piera snapped as he noticed Inkeri had opened her mouth, ready to speak, then he stood up to his full height. 'It's not like before the war. It's just not, and it never will be again. What we had before is in the past now. Of what's to come, we have only an inkling, if that. That's what the birds losing their minds really means. The animals know it fine well. They're not stupid. Animals are far from stupid. It's us humans that have the tendency for that.'

Inkeri looked at him.

'Right, the path's clear. On you come.'

Inkeri stood in the protection of her oiled coat, looked down, bit her lip, swallowed her words and gingerly stepped along the path Piera had cleared. She reached the old man at a spot where

94

mugs and shards of glass, knives and forks lay scattered on the ground. Inkeri's heart leapt up her throat from nervousness, but at the same time she felt a shred of disappointment. Was this it? Was there nothing else? Though, of course, even this was more than nothing. This was closer to the truth than she had ever been, yet she was still somehow disappointed. No. She had not found any documents lying hidden beneath the mud. Of course she hadn't. There was no trace of Kaarlo.

She picked up one of the mugs. Piera continued swinging the cumbersome-looking machine and turned his head to one side, the better to hear the beeps. Inkeri watched his movements, looked at the mug in her hand, deflated, but took a photograph of it all the same. A memory of the image was burnt into the film. A swallow had been drawn on to the side of the mug, on the bottom was the insignia from the Arabia ceramics factory in Helsinki. Inkeri felt a chill. She knew that Kaarlo hadn't enjoyed being here. He loved Kenya, its warmth, its raw, abundant nature. He loved dressing up in a three-piece suit, always placing a handkerchief of his liking in his breast pocket, and he wore colourful bow ties and laughed freely. God, how she missed that laughter, so happy and innocent. Kaarlo had a somewhat decrepit frame, yet his youthful, good-humoured behaviour never failed to make even the servants smile. Inkeri was suddenly filled with a surge of grief and shame. She gulped back the tears. For a woman, even a single tear, a single show of weakness, was too much.

'What happened to the prisoners after the war?' she asked, clearing her throat. Piera stopped swinging the metal detector and looked at her.

'Don't know. There was talk about evacuating them, but if you ask me, I suspect most of 'em were executed up here. Or sent to Norway first and killed there, no doubt.'

Inkeri felt a chill down her spine. With her hand in her pocket, she gripped Kaarlo's photograph in her fist and wondered if she dared show it to him. She didn't know Piera well enough yet. She didn't know how people might react to such things. Everything was uncertain. She swallowed and felt the aftertaste of anxiety.

'Did you ever see this man? Take a good look,' she said quickly, her voice almost impatient. Piera walked towards her, took the photograph and scrutinized it. His wrinkly hands were steady. His expression did not flinch, but his eyes lingered on the image for a long while.

'Was he a prisoner?'

Inkeri did not answer.

Piera looked at her and licked his lips. 'Who is he?'

'If you don't know, perhaps you know someone who might have more information about him?'

'The Nazis,' he chuckled, and began stuffing tobacco into his pipe. 'Most of 'em are behind bars now, either that or they were executed. You must know that.'

'Is there no paperwork? Nothing at all? Not even among the Finnish documents?' Inkeri implored him, though she already knew the answer. All conversations that she had had with the authorities about papers and documentation had been woeful. There was no information about anything. Nothing but disinterested expressions, comments designed to let her know that this was none of her business, that she should be grateful for what she had. We should focus on the future. Why did everybody keep saying that to her? Was it even true? There was still so much in the past to discover. The past was all around, though people tried to hide it with the smell of freshly cut wood and some electric lights. And yet, there was so terribly little that was new, that was truly hers and hers alone. The only person who had agreed to help her was her childhood friend Lotta Niinistö, who had worked as an agent during the war and who had eventually shown Inkeri some maps and told her of her suspicions. Without Lotta, she would never have known what little she knew about Kaarlo's fate.

Piera handed the photograph back to her. 'The fact of the matter is, the Finnish authorities didn't have much to do with these camps. They weren't our camps; they were the Germans' camps. The police just tried to make sure the camps upheld Finnish law, and of course that wasn't always the case.'

'Is there no living Finn with knowledge of what went on here?'

Piera was quiet and looked up at the sky. His cap fluttered in the wind. Eventually he gave a sigh. 'I visited the camp quite a few times, taking food and what have you. Sometimes I saw locals there: cooks, interpreters, soldiers, police…'

At the mention of the police, Inkeri raised an eyebrow. Lotta Niinistö had told her that certain officers had conducted reconnaissance and espionage operations on the orders of the state police.

'Do you know the names of these authorities? A policeman, perhaps?'

Piera thought back; he seemed to be choosing his words carefully.

'There was one police officer up here.'

'And his name?'

'Let me think… The name of the chief of police was Tapani something… Tapani… Koskela, that was it!'

'Tapani Koskela. Do you know if he is still working?'

'No, I don't think so. Well, how would I know? I don't know anything about these matters,' he hissed, then paused. 'But I do know he was up here right at the very end of the war. Brought prisoners with him too, he did.'

'Why didn't anybody tell me this before?' Inkeri reproached him like a disappointed child.

Piera's gaze was deep and intense. The curved fold of his cap suddenly returned to its correct position as he quickly looked up at her. 'What's that supposed to mean?'

'I mean all this. That there was a prison camp here after all… Everything.'

Piera finally stood to his full height and switched off his machine again. He lit his pipe, sniffed and looked straight ahead. Inkeri felt a shiver.

'I've got a question for you too. Why are you so interested?'

'Why shouldn't I be?'

'Because nobody's interested,' he replied, his voice lowered, and stared her in the eye for so long that Inkeri eventually had to look away. He puffed on his pipe. Droplets trickled along his wrinkles. 'I've always said that questions of faith are between me and this here mountain,' he said quietly and calmly. 'And so are these questions. Understood?' He propped his leg on a small boulder and leant against his knee. 'You see, one thing I've learnt is that outsiders don't give a damn about this land unless there's something in it for them. Don't get me wrong, now. But you, Mrs Lindqvist, you're an outsider.'

Once he had finished, he straightened his back, turned to his machine and switched it on again, then continued looking for scrap metal in peace and quiet. Inkeri was unable to utter a word. She could hardly breathe. She felt small tears trickling down her cheeks and wiped them away, trying to convince herself it was only melting snow. She turned and made to leave.

'Watch your step, mind. And Inkeri,' said Piera, quickly turning to face her. 'I hope you find your man.' Then he returned to his work.

INARI

Mar. 1944

WE HAVE STARTED making our way back. Thirty kilometres as the crow flies, but we have been forced to take a detour through the village of Inari, where we arrived yesterday.

We are staying with a local Sámi woman. Her name is Biret-Ánne, and Heiskanen told me that not only is this old *áhkku* the richest woman in the village, but she is the richest person overall, that during the war some people have made it rich like you wouldn't believe. The woman's room is filled with handicrafts and silverware, spoons, traditional cradle-ball charms and goblets made of reindeer antlers, which she sells to the Germans at an inflated price.

Biret-Ánne was there to meet us; in her gleaming new fur coat she looked vigorous and self-assured. I heard that she also hosts the German gentry and makes sure there are always locals in Sámi costume to wait on tables and perform for the guests. 'She supplies whores too,' Heiskanen whispered in my ear and winked.

At Biret-Ánne's inn we ate what must have been the best meal of the entire trip. Reindeer and dried meat. We were served real liquor too, though for the others she only offered Hoffmann's drops. My word, it tasted good.

Today is our day of rest.

The soldiers visit Biret-Ánne's inn to buy souvenirs. The lives of these nomadic peoples are so peculiar, so alien. Imagine that such indigenous people still exist to this day, tribes that haven't developed beyond the hunting and gathering phase.

I saw Heiskanen and Saara outside the canteen, as I was taking care of some affairs at Inari parish church. It took me by surprise. They appeared to be arguing about something. I watched them for a good fifteen minutes. When Heiskanen left, I ran up to the bloodletter and spoke to her. At first she pretended not to recognize me, feigned being in a rush, but I didn't give in.

'Ah yes, *that* Väinö. Väinö Remes,' she said, and looked right at me with that piercing stare of hers. I managed to ask if I might offer her coffee and cake, seeing as we were right in front of the canteen, and after a small silence, to my great surprise, she consented.

Once we had sat at the café table for a moment in silence, I plucked up the courage to ask what exactly she and Heiskanen had been talking about. Saara looked at me from beneath her furrowed brow and gave a squawking laugh.

'You really want to know?' she asked. I looked around.

'Yes, I do,' I replied, though I was beginning to feel afraid of what I might hear.

Saara explained that she had asked for some gauzes for the female prisoners. When they bleed, women smell dreadful when they have no opportunity to wash or change their rags.

Heiskanen was reluctant to put in an order. Saara explained the matter vehemently, her eyes fixed on me all the while. I listened to her calmly, without once interrupting. When I didn't react in the least, she squirmed in her chair and tried to think what to say next. Suddenly her eyes brightened.

'Would you do it for me?' And just then she touched my hand as it rested on the table. The way she looked me in the eyes made the bottom of my stomach lurch.

How can anyone say no to eyes like those?

Mar. 1944

The day before we left, we packed up our belongings, and Biret-Ánne even gave us some dried meat to take with us in the sled. 'Around here the only thing the reindeer leave behind is their spirit,' she laughed in that familiar, shrill old voice. We exchanged some German marks and bought stamps and writing paper.

Heiskanen looked at the stamps, which showed an image commemorating the alliance between Finland and the Germans. He muttered to himself, then growled at Biret-Ánne. 'Is this propaganda all you have?'

'We've got stamps with Mannerheim and Ryti too if you prefer,' she blurted out. Heiskanen raised his eyebrows, took the stamps, the writing paper and the money. The old woman chuckled about how, before the war, her family in Nuorgam didn't even realize they were considered Finnish. 'In the olden days there used to be a customs office in southern Lapland, leagues away from the national borders. Well, nowadays they probably think they're Germans instead,' she said, carefully counted the marks twice, then handed us the money.

Once back in the village, I bumped into the bloodletter again. We wouldn't necessarily have said anything to each other if I hadn't seen something so extraordinary that I stood gawping on the spot.

'What's happened to you, Väinö Remes?' she asked, though I could see she would much rather have walked right past me. I pointed upwards.

Floating across the sky were clouds tinged in pastel colours, like pearls. Instinctively, I grabbed Saara and held her in my arms; she laughed and asked what on earth had come over me. I told her that the clouds could be a sign of danger, a lethal new gas perhaps. 'Who knows?' But Saara laughed and repeated my name in a tone of amused rebuke.

'We call it a Finnmark cloud,' she whispered into my ear. I felt the moist warmth of her breath, and we looked on as the pearly cloud glistened at the highest point in the sky.

Mar. 1944

Before leaving, I was ordered to take two German guards to the county jail. We let them out of the sled by the church. I don't know exactly what they are supposed to have done, but their final mistake was trying to give the prisoners some extra food.

I suppose I recognized him from the creak of the floorboards in the jail. I don't know how one can identify a person from something like that. The way that, just before a storm, there is an ear-splitting silence. Everybody always talks about that silence, but to me it feels more as though time stops still, as though it doesn't exist at all. It must surely be an instinct of some sort, an animalistic sense. At first, of course, I thought I had seen a ghost. We hadn't seen each other since the eastern front. Since Alakurtti in 1942, to be precise.

And, of course, Tapani Koskela recognized me too straight away, though he commented, 'There's a changed man if ever I saw one.'

ENONTEKIÖ, 1948

O LAVI WAS STANDING in the clear, frozen air and looking both at the tall fig tree and at Inkeri's puzzled expression. Severed fish heads dangled from the branches of the trees in front of the house, and she had been expressing concern about them for some time. 'We make them into chowder for the dogs during the winter,' Olavi explained, though Inkeri's face remained unchanged. She was puzzled.

'How shall we ever get that thing home in one piece?' she asked as she sized up the tree. Olavi had no idea. He had first heard of the fig plant when he was helping to evacuate people during the fighting in Lapland. Almost in jest, he'd once said that if the plant survived the war and ended up without a home, he would take care of it. The owner had died, but Olavi's wishes hadn't been forgotten, and now he was at a loss as to how to transport the plant home.

He and Inkeri had already tried to fit the plant into the back seat in so many different ways that they were almost out of ideas. There was no other option but to prop it between them and hope for the best. When Olavi turned the key in the ignition, the engine sputtered into life and the car proceeded to jolt up and down with every pothole as they pulled away, and the entire undertaking was beginning to seem doomed to failure. They were in for a most unpleasant journey. They looked at the row of fells up ahead.

'Did you know these fells used to be the size of the Alps? Erosion has worn them down. Their rounded shape is unique to these parts. From the top of a fell the view is very different from when you're surrounded by tall mountains. Here you can see into the distance. And the flowers that grow on these fells are very rare. As soon as the snow melts, the flowers push through the ground in less than a week. The blossoming season is short. Sometimes it lasts two weeks, sometimes even less. Plants normally go to sleep at night. But these plants are awake all through the summer. They have a thirst for life. And they need it; they have such a short time to live,' Olavi mused. Inkeri looked at him, perplexed. He shrugged his shoulders. 'What?' he laughed. 'That moment when the flowers across the fell blossom all at once, that's something you don't see every day. You might never see it. But when you do, you'll never forget it.'

Inkeri looked at him and smiled. After a few turns in the road, they arrived at a crossroads where they were stopped by the police. Olavi parked the car and the police stepped out of their vehicle.

'Afternoon.'

'Good afternoon,' Inkeri replied. Olavi stared straight ahead. The police looked at the plant.

'What's that?'

'A fig tree,' said Inkeri. The officers laughed at the plant. Olavi's gaze did not budge. She took his sudden stiffness for nerves about the fate of the tree. 'Surely it's not prohibited?' she asked.

'We'll let it go. Have you got any identification? There are smugglers here up to no good. We're checking everybody's papers.'

'Of course,' Inkeri replied cheerfully, and took her passport from the glove compartment. One of the officers examined it and raised an eyebrow.

'Fine picture you have here, ma'am,' he said, and held it up. Olavi turned to look at it. It certainly was a fine picture. It must have been about twenty years old and taken at a proper studio. Inkeri was in an elegant dress, her hair was beautifully styled, and she was wearing jewellery, lipstick too, her head turned gracefully to one side. Inkeri laughed. The policeman's eyes lingered on her.

'And you, sir?'

Olavi reached into his pocket, took out a card and handed it to the officer.

'This has seen better days,' the officer muttered, held the document at arm's length and squinted at the picture. 'Do you have a better passport, sir?'

'I'm afraid not. A military passport, but I don't carry it around with me. I'd happily never see it again.'

'We can certainly agree on that,' the officer chuckled and showed the picture to his colleague.

What a mess, Olavi heard the officers' conversation. *It's high time we did something about these old passports. Look at the state of this one.* Then the officer who had taken the passport handed it back to him, doffed his cap and wished them a pleasant afternoon. The two officers walked back to their police car and started the engine. Olavi waited for the car to disappear from view. He took a deep breath, turned the ignition and tried to hide the fact that his hands were trembling. He had only been driving for a moment when the car swerved out of his control. Luckily, they weren't travelling at speed, and the car came to a halt at the edge of the road, its side tight against the snowy embankment.

'What on earth was that? I thought you said you could drive!' Inkeri gasped, but from behind the fig tree Olavi could see only a small glimpse of her.

'I can,' he grumbled, and switched off the engine.

'What are you doing?' she shouted. Olavi didn't answer but continued to grip the steering wheel with both hands.

'Olavi! Switch the engine on right now! It's minus thirty degrees. I'm going to freeze. And so will you. It's at least twenty kilometres to the nearest village.' Inkeri sounded almost frantic.

Olavi lowered his head and thought hard.

'At the very least, the fig will die if you don't do anything! There's only an hour of daylight left!'

Olavi took off his hat and wiped the sweat from his hairline, then pulled out his cigarettes and lighter. Inkeri stared at him in bewilderment. He held out the box of cigarettes, waited for her slender fingers to take one, then closed it again. They listened to the silence around them.

'Piera tells me you're looking for your husband.'

Inkeri glanced at him, astounded. When Piera told him about the incident at the worksite, Olavi was annoyed that Piera had gone and told her about Koskela. Piera defended himself, asking what else he could have done. She'll find out sooner or later, he argued, and if they gave her at least something to go on, some little clue, perhaps she wouldn't pester them with questions all the time. In that respect the old man was right, Olavi admitted to himself. But he could play that game too, and besides, there was always the small chance that Bigga had misunderstood everything in the first place. Hope was something it was very hard to let go of.

'Why are you looking for him?'

Inkeri turned to Olavi, agog, then closed her mouth and puffed furiously on her cigarette. The windows steamed up.

'Because he might not be dead.'

'What do you mean?' Olavi asked, trying to conceal the growing agitation in his voice.

She looked at him. 'What's it to you?'

'Well, it would certainly explain what you're doing up here,' he said quietly.

'It's none of your business what I'm doing here!'

'Maybe I can help.'

Inkeri turned to look at him and scoffed.

'You don't have many options. I might be your best chance. Do you think anyone is going to be interested in a missing prisoner of war?' Olavi asked.

'Very well. He... He was... He was taken prisoner, the entire troop were taken prisoner or died, and those who survived were transported to a camp in the Soviet Union. A group of prisoners managed to escape the camp. Kaarlo was among them. It seems he succeeded in crossing the border, because one way or another he got back to the Finnish side. But he was recaptured and taken to one of the Nazi camps. First the camp at Inari, then the one at Enontekiö.'

'How do you know all this?' he said.

'I've seen the detention and prisoner logs, and his name is mentioned in the Red Cross's list of prisoners from the Lapland camps.'

'The Red Cross…' Olavi began quietly, then laughed quietly. *Of course.* 'Where did you get hold of those?' he asked, now rather more sceptical. It was an extraordinary admission.

'Why are you so interested? Do you know something about him?' Inkeri pressed.

'You haven't answered my question. Why are you looking for him?'

'Because he might be alive,' she repeated. 'Isn't that enough?'

'It's been many years since then,' said Olavi, lowering his voice. Inkeri's posture seemed to melt and she turned away in annoyance. Tobacco smoke engulfed them. Tiny little stars had appeared in the sky.

'What else can I do?' she whispered. 'I have nothing left.'

'Piera gave you the name of a man who might know something about him.'

'Yes,' she stammered.

'Koskela?'

'That's right. Tapani Koskela.'

'Have you found out anything about him?'

'No. Not yet. Do you know anything about him?'

'I know who he is…' Olavi conceded.

'Tell me!' she shouted. Olavi looked at her. Her expression was at once panicked and self-assured. Olavi thought for a moment. He thought about what was right, then thought about what might be the safest option, the option most beneficial to him. In many ways, the two did not align. He had to make a choice. Even very unlikely things can sometimes be true.

'Tapani Koskela might well know something, but I don't think he will be of much use.'

'How do you know that?' Inkeri snapped.

'I just know,' he replied curtly.

'Do *you* know what happened to my husband after the war?'

Olavi was quiet, wiped the windowpane with his sleeve. 'I'll answer you, and I'll tell you the truth, but I won't answer a second time, and you won't ask me ever again. Understood?'

'Understood,' Inkeri whispered. Ice crystals had begun to form on her eyelashes.

'No. I do not know what became of your husband after the war, and I'm not involved in any way,' he said, then swallowed, but didn't look away. 'But there is one person who does know. Of that I'm certain.'

'Who?'

'The bloodletter. *Noaidi*. She worked at the camp as a cupper and a nurse.' Olavi paused and thought once more about how to continue. The decision had been made. He could no longer change course. He licked his chapped lips.

'Who is she? Where can I find her?'

'Nobody knows where she is,' he replied, and wondered how to phrase it so as not to reveal anything about himself. 'Piera said that your husband was brought here in the final days of the war. Is that right?'

'It says so in the prisoner log,' Inkeri nodded.

'The bloodletter is known to have been here in the last days of the war. If you can locate her or find out what happened to her, I am sure you'll find out what happened to your husband too. She was often involved in the transportation of prisoners.' Olavi's expression was bright, his gaze fixed on Inkeri's eyes. She was trembling, either with cold or something else. Probably something else.

'What is her name?' she asked impatiently.

'Saara.'

'What?'

'Saara. Her name is Saara Valva,' said Olavi, and he cleared his throat then lowered his head. All of a sudden he heard birdsong. Inkeri looked up too. A robin, perhaps, or something else. Maybe a redpoll. There was something plaintive about its twittering.

'Strange. They don't normally sing at this time of day. Not in that way,' Olavi mumbled, lost in thought. Inkeri furrowed her brow. The sounds all disappeared and silence fell. Olavi patted his pockets, then tried the keys in the ignition.

'How do you know these people?' Inkeri asked sternly. Olavi thought about this.

'I used to work with them during the war. I can't tell you any more than that. You don't need to know any more. I can't be of any use to you.'

'You used to work with them? What do you mean by that? Like Piera?'

Olavi knew that a good lie was one that stuck as closely as possible to the truth. 'Yes, just like Piera,' he said, and started the car.

INARI

Mar. 1944

ONCE WE HAD LEFT, Heiskanen asked me about Koskela. I muttered something vague and tried to change the subject. The old Sámi crone is typical of these indigenous people: small, dwarfish and very superstitious, and it is hard to understand why she gets on with the Nazis as well as she does.

'She doesn't really,' Heiskanen quipped, and explained that the Nazis had a very begrudging relationship with the Lapps. They had been taught that these primitive northern hunter-gatherer peoples were a relic, the genetic dregs left behind by human civilization, that they were defined as an evolutionary anomaly caused by the prevailing environmental circumstances.

I nodded in agreement, commenting that the peoples living in these northern frontier areas are a completely different race from us Finns. 'Even Väinö Lassila from the League for Human Rights has proved through his skull examinations that these Sámi countryfolk belong to the lower races,' I said, trying to muster a brisk, energetic tone of voice.

Heiskanen squinted and glanced at me. He seemed to hesitate before saying: 'Precisely, just like the bloodletter.'

On the way home, two prisoners escaped—on my watch. Heiskanen saw it happen, and so did Kalle. We have been ordered to shoot whenever anybody tries to escape, but I've never shot anybody before. It has never been part of my duties. I don't know what happened. Perhaps nothing, perhaps everything, but for some reason I simply couldn't get the weapon out of its holster, and everything happened very quickly. Heiskanen was the one who took the shot, but he missed. I just stood by, gawping inanely. I felt embarrassed and ashamed. We were far enough away from the rest of the group that nobody noticed anything. Heiskanen quickly grabbed me and told me to continue on my way as if nothing had happened. He ordered Kalle to run back to the other prisoners and tell them we'd shot a reindeer that had stepped on a mine. He obeyed, though he was weak. It wasn't until we were walking half an hour behind the others that I managed to open my mouth, but nothing came out. It was only then that I noticed my hands were trembling.

At some point, Heiskanen stopped me and shoved me against a tree. He looked me right in the eye, told me I mustn't breathe a word about this to anybody, said he would take care of the paperwork to make sure everything tallied up and see to it that any discrepancies couldn't be tied to us. He offered me a cigarette, lit it, then gave me a generous gulp of liquor from his hip flask and a few drops of medication from a small phial. 'Swallow it, you're quivering like a leaf,' he said. The substance took effect almost instantly. The trembling stopped.

An hour or so later I was able to speak again. Black clouds above the horizon.

'Looks like rain,' I said, and drew fresh tobacco smoke into my lungs.

'Yes, snowfall,' said Heiskanen.

'We'll have summer rain soon,' I continued, and swallowed. I closed my eyes.

'Before that, the snow will melt, the sun will shine, and we'll be able to swim and fish out in the lake,' said Heiskanen.

We said nothing more. Heiskanen began quietly whistling a wartime *Schlager*; life was miserable, but his spirit hadn't died. Further off, I heard someone tell a joke and one of the prisoners laughing. The soldiers' weapons slapped rhythmically against their backsides, swinging casually like forgotten shackles.

In the trees, the birds sang through the translucent silence. Their song was peace.

Apr. 1944

I couldn't sleep last night. I sat awake in the shelter, smoking and looking at the stars. Suddenly, I heard something close by. I reached for my weapon. In the glow of the fire, I saw a reindeer step out of the darkness. Even at a distance, I could tell it was a decrepit old thing. It looked at me with large eyes, its antlers reaching up towards the sky. It stood there for a long while and didn't seem frightened of me, though reindeer are normally very timid animals indeed. I looked at the creature until it turned and left, disappeared into the white forest.

Apr. 1944

We arrived back at the camp yesterday.

As soon as he woke up, Heiskanen came to tell me that everything was in order and I didn't have to worry that the prisoners had escaped. I asked how he had sorted it out. He didn't reply. All he said was that he had taken care of the matter, but I got the distinct impression that he had embroiled me in something I would rather not be embroiled in.

Apr. 1944

Around midday, I noticed that the bloodletter had returned to the camp too. She arrived more quickly this time, because she'd travelled by car. When I looked at her she didn't avert her eyes.

And I looked at her for a long time.

II

INARI

Apr. 1944

I T IS PEACEFUL, and the weather is mild. There are more animal tracks in the surrounding terrain than there have been for a long time. Soon the flowers will start to blossom. The plants here have xerophyte qualities. Their flowers are small, they have strong root systems and a wax-like coating on their leaves. In this way they maximize the nutrients they get from the scant Lappish light.

Apr. 1944

I've started spending more and more time with the bloodletter. I have borrowed books on local flora from the camp's library, books that Heiskanen has ordered. Saara laughs at how passionately I read about plants, but she asks me about them all the while. She finds my enthusiasm rather endearing. When I asked her why, at first she refused to answer.

Eventually she said that, when I am reading, I look more like myself.

I revealed to Saara that I recently came across an old acquaintance. I told her about Koskela. Saara said she knew the man well, that the two of them visit other camps too, conducting various operations. Or raids. Mostly raids. Apparently, the police regularly examine the homes of any local women who live alone. Married women are left in peace. Saara explained that if there is the slightest suggestion that a woman is living a promiscuous lifestyle—and a simple complaint from a jealous neighbour is generally enough to arouse suspicions—the woman is forced to have an internal examination. Saara conducts these examinations. And if any of the women is with child, but doesn't have proof of a Finnish father, she is locked up immediately or sent directly to a labour camp. Venereal disease is enough to warrant conviction too.

Saara didn't ask me, or perhaps she did, I can't remember, but I told her about my own past. I told her how well I remembered the moment when, standing at Kajaani coach station waiting for the bus, I got my first good look at Tapani Koskela. He was wearing a peaked cap. I felt nervous but excited. We were on our way into occupied territories to complete an important task. We were to re-establish a Greater Finland.

I told her how strange it felt to see Koskela in charge of the local jail. And what a jail it is! The cells are full of German prisoners. There are so many of them that almost all the local jails in Lapland have been forced to let go of their Finnish prisoners, who in turn have been transferred to the provincial jails in Oulu and Kainuu. 'Incredible,' I muttered. Saara laughed.

'For the Nazis, the only thing worse than the lower races is race betrayal. Nazis who fornicate with degenerates are executed at six o'clock every Sunday morning.'

Apr. 1944

The birds start singing at five in the morning, then have an hour's break after eight. Today, breathing feels somehow easier, lighter.

The length of daylight is sixteen hours and seventeen minutes.

Apr. 1944

Today I saw Heiskanen talking to Saara. They were laughing at something. I don't know what. And when Heiskanen lowered his hand, he brushed it against the bloodletter's left arm, as if by accident, and nothing has ever hurt me more than this.

Apr. 1944

Ten prisoners have managed to escape. Kalle among them.

ENONTEKIÖ, 1949

O LAVI SAT on the bench in the living room and waited. In front of him was a flowerpot, half filled with soil. He had run out of energy. The grandfather clock was ticking, but otherwise it was quiet, and there were no sounds from outside either. He looked around the silent room. Over the past year, Inkeri had put her stamp on the living room, so much so that he found it hard to remember it ever looking any different. In Inkeri's bedroom, which was to the left of the living room and whose door stood open, there was a small screen. Inkeri had painted it herself, or rather the pupils from the school had painted it. Beside it stood another screen, this one slightly lighter in colour, and both were leaning against a set of black lights that Inkeri had somehow acquired from Norway. Not only that, she had managed to get hold of a Zorki camera from the Soviet Union and another camera from the United States. She had reviewed them for a magazine read by professional photographers, but Olavi didn't have the faintest understanding of their different qualities.

Inkeri's bedroom had the most natural light of any room in the house, and because it was next to the living room, this had become almost an extension of her own room. The large wooden table had been all but commandeered for putting the finishing touches to her photographs, fixing them, enhancing and signing them. A pile of images lay strewn across the table now.

The front door suddenly opened.

'Snow coming in from the north,' Piera called out, and hung his blue cap on the hook by the stove. 'And the Northern Lights were so bright, even the ice was sparkling!'

'Where the hell have you been?' Olavi growled. Piera had set off before the New Year to visit family in Sweden and Norway, picking up goods everywhere he went.

'Had to pay a visit to the border guards,' Piera muttered. On the damp, soil-covered table he laid a small wallet filled with Swedish öre and placed three bottles of liquor beside it.

Olavi looked at the bounty. 'I thought I'd paid for more than that.'

'That's how much I got for the money.'

'You used to get more.'

'That was then. Now is now. The laws have tightened. The shipment's safe, but it's not something you want to do too often.'

'Who was the bootlegger?' Olavi enquired as Piera began counting out the money.

'Didn't know him. Some old boy from the Swedish side… One of Inkeri's contacts,' he mumbled, then began unpacking his wares on the table: sugar, coffee, flour and a bag clearly containing clothes. Aid packages from the Finnish Red Cross had become smaller throughout the previous year, and eventually they had stopped altogether. The change was apparent in the sheer selection of products illegally shipped across the borders. It was clear that Inkeri had decided to settle here permanently, and now she too had started sending some of her bootlegged goods to the south. She had even had clothes mended in Helsinki, then sold them at the market in Rovaniemi on her return journey. Still, she always brought the best things back here. Young women, and young men too, had started to show a greater interest in different kinds of clothes and shoes, and Inkeri had become popular with the local youngsters. The school was every bit as good a marketplace as Rovaniemi.

In addition, across the border in Sweden Inkeri had found a smuggler who sold them Brazilian coffee and liquor of average quality. This had caused an immediate flurry of interest, if not in everybody then in close to ninety per cent of the villagers. In the past, coffee used to be available on the Norwegian coast, and much of it came from Brazil. After the war, however, the closed borders meant that people had to make do with coffee substitutes. It was still impossible to buy coffee from the grocer's. When Inkeri brought her first batch across the border and the villagers got a taste of real coffee and liquor, she was finally accepted into the community. By now people liked her more than they did Olavi.

'What are you going to do with all that money?' Olavi asked, and examined the purse. 'You might have family in Sweden, but even you haven't got permission to keep that many *öre* on you.'

'Well… The police let me keep just enough to get over to the Swedish side for coffee and cake. On this side of the border, anything more than that will land you in the clink.'

'That wasn't an answer,' Olavi snapped, but he helped Piera count the remaining money one more time. Piera stared at Olavi's hands and looked at the mess on the table.

'I'm repotting these.'

'Repotting, indeed?'

'When will I get the rest?'

'Next week, then the week after that.'

'What about Inkeri's delivery?'

'Same thing.'

Olavi suddenly rose to his feet and picked up a pile of letters from the table.

'Here.'

'What are these?' Piera croaked.

'A few new stamps for your collection. Inkeri gets post almost every week.'

Piera chuckled and lifted one of the envelopes up to the light. The stamp showed the image of a man carrying a heavy load of bricks on his back.

'The Lapland reconstruction stamp! Now I've got the whole set,' Piera beamed, and handed the envelope back to Olavi. 'You keep 'em. I don't collect these any more. I stopped when my folder started filling up with Nazi stamps, swastikas, Finnish Hackapelites and soldiers waging war against the east,' he said, and stepped back, dragging his bags with him. 'Put 'em next to the national aid stamp, the one with the picture of Lapland in ruins.'

Olavi shrugged his shoulders.

'Fair enough. I thought it might interest you,' he muttered.

There was a faint mist outside. It was smoke. Logs were crackling in the hearth, giving off steam. Piera looked around; he hadn't visited the house for a year.

'What's that?' he asked, and pointed at the shelf. Olavi turned to look.

'A gramophone.'

'And what about that?'

Olavi's eyes followed Piera's finger.

'They're records. They play music.'

'I know that. I mean that thing.' And Olavi looked at the large box that had stood next to the sofa for a long time and that Inkeri hadn't yet touched.

'It's a camera. Takes pictures in colour apparently, but it's broken. Who knows?'

'Well, well,' Piera muttered under his breath.

'Have you had a peek inside the darkroom?'

'I'll have to take a look,' said Piera. 'But I did come here for a reason. You know the old saying that you shouldn't put all your eggs in one basket?'

'I do.'

'Now there's a stupid saying if ever I heard one.'

'Yes…?'

'But it's true all the same.'

Olavi sighed, flicked his lighter and lit a cigarette, and scratched the green paint from under the corner of the table as he waited for Piera to get to the point. The manufacturer's initials had been carved into the underside of the wood. A long line curving in a semicircle. After that, though he ran his fingers along it, he couldn't make out the text. These were Cyrillic letters. The walls of the plywood tents at the camp had been covered in similar scrawls. Яков / 22 / Красное село / Нарва. Инари. Name, age, battlefields, end point. The words always ended for the same reason: death.

'So I wondered if I might leave some of the goods here,' Piera asked eventually. Olavi looked out of the window and saw a low cloud of smoke floating past. There would be a blizzard soon.

'Did you buy this from one of the prisoners?' he asked quietly and tapped the tabletop.

'Aye. A skinny little Serb. Good table too.'

'It is that.' *It is that.* Olavi listened as the grandfather clock chimed beside him. Sprawling in the corner of the room, the fig now stood over two metres tall, its leaves reaching up towards the window. A bottle of milk had been left on the table from breakfast; the light had soured it. Sunlight filtered through the smoke.

'By all means,' Olavi agreed. Piera nodded, looked him in the eye, then stared at the empty bottles on the table.

'Áddjá!' came a voice from the hallway. It was Bigga-Marja. Neither of them had heard the front door opening.

'Well, I'll be damned!' Piera shouted, and hugged the girl as she ran into her grandfather's arms.

'What are you doing here?' Bigga asked.

'What are *you* doing here?'

'Inkeri said I could come here after school and watch how to develop photographs. The ones we took in Helsinki,' Bigga enthused. 'Hasn't she come back yet?'

'I'm sure she'll be here soon. Now, tell me all about Helsinki,' said Piera. Bigga-Marja was supposed to have accompanied Inkeri to Helsinki before Christmas, but because she wasn't able to travel without a passport, the journey had to be postponed. All year, Bigga-Marja had shown a growing interest in Inkeri's lessons and especially in photography. Eventually, Inkeri had started teaching her how to take photographs after class. Bigga had become very good at it. She had even accompanied Inkeri on a few work trips. Inkeri had started to wonder if she might employ her as her official assistant. And that is what gave her the idea to take the girl to Helsinki so she could meet the paper's editor-in-chief.

Naturally, Bigga-Marja was thrilled and hadn't been able to think about anything else for weeks. After the trip, however, Olavi had noticed that she seemed rather downcast, quieter than usual.

'*Got dat manai?*' Piera asked again, this time in Sámi.

'*Dat manai ihán bures…*' Bigga mumbled, and began fiddling with the ribbons on her sleeves. Piera raised his eyebrows. With some reluctance, Bigga-Marja told him that Helsinki had been full of people staring and pointing at her. Melander, the newspaper's chief editor, hadn't allowed her to work as Inkeri's assistant, and Inkeri had received a strange letter that she'd read over and over.

'And she mentioned Saara's name,' said Bigga-Marja.

'Did she indeed?' Piera muttered, and glanced at Olavi, who was pouring himself another drink.

'What else was in the letter?' Piera asked, and popped his pipe into his mouth.

'Don't know.'

'Well, what else did Inkeri tell you?'

'Nothing. She didn't seem worried or anything.' Bigga spoke quietly, looked up at the ceiling and sniffed. 'But we're going to Pallas together next week.'

'You've become a real photographer too then?'

'Yes!' she laughed.

Piera and Bigga-Marja continued their conversation in Sámi. Olavi concentrated on his mug. He sighed and rubbed his eyes. It was only a matter of time before Inkeri got the chance to speak to Koskela. Olavi knew that Koskela was a sensible, intelligent man, but could he be sure the policeman would keep his name out of it? Koskela might blurt out something small, something insignificant, but something that might cause Inkeri to start looking into Olavi's past more closely.

'Why is Inkeri so interested in Saara?' Bigga-Marja asked suddenly.

'Because she thinks Saara might know something about her husband,' Olavi grunted.

'How will investigating Saara help with that?' Bigga asked, her expression puzzled. Just then the front door opened. All three of them gave a start.

But Inkeri gave a breezy *hello* from the hallway and Bigga-Marja ran straight for the darkroom, where she could hear Inkeri heading too. Piera followed her, eager to see this famous room for himself. Olavi remained alone in the living room, staring at the creaking door as it closed behind them.

INARI

May 1944

TODAY, SAARA and I passed each other without saying a word, but when I closed the barn door and, though not among my normal duties, began giving the horses their hay, there she suddenly was. She took two steps towards me. She stood right in front of me, first laid her head against my chest, sniffed my shirt, my sweat, then ran her teeth along the bare skin at the point where the torso meets the neck. Then she took my hand in hers, moved it beneath her skirt and pressed it between her legs, and I felt how wet she was, how warm and soft was the skin of her inner thighs, and that too so moist.

May 1944

I've been looking for the escaped prisoners. We still haven't located all of them. Perhaps they are hiding in the locals' houses, perhaps high up in the fells. The latter is more likely. We have handed our information over to the police.

Heiskanen is worried about Kalle. The mare hasn't been eating properly since he disappeared.

ENONTEKIÖ, 1949

BIGGA-MARJA STOOD in the cold outdoor air staring at the horizon. Because Inkeri didn't dare drive the car in the frozen weather they had taken the bus, which left them at the end of the path leading up to the hotel. Inkeri had brought the girl along to write an article about the newly rebuilt Pallas Hotel. This would be Bigga-Marja's first proper newspaper article. Inkeri had allowed her to write a few questions that she could ask the hotel guests and promised her she could take some photographs of her own too.

'Be careful not to let the lens freeze up or the film snap. It's cold out here,' Bigga reminded Inkeri as she focused her camera on the horizon. Of course, Inkeri smirked to herself. Bigga had already managed to break her practice camera. At first the lens had frosted up as normal, but then air had breached the seal and frozen the lens from the inside too. Once back in the warm, the frost then condensed into water and soaked both the lens and the mechanism. Inkeri propped her sunglasses on her forehead. She had been teaching Bigga-Marja how to use the camera, given her advice about exposure times and other technical considerations. She had shown her how to keep her arms elevated so her grip didn't slacken. Sometimes you had to examine the subject of the photograph for a long time, she explained, you have to find a suitable angle, a suitable moment, suitable light. And your hands mustn't tremble, particularly not with a long exposure time.

Though the two had spent a lot of time together, Inkeri still found Bigga-Marja somewhat distant; it was as though the girl was constantly on edge and didn't really trust her. Now Inkeri suddenly noticed a dark figure wandering along the amber blaze of the horizon.

'*Nulpu ja heargi*,' Bigga gasped. Inkeri gave her a curious look. 'A male and female reindeer,' Bigga explained. Inkeri took the sunglasses from her eyes to get a better look. 'Why do you wear those glasses in the wintertime?' she asked.

'Well,' Inkeri smiled. 'I love the light, but unfortunately it doesn't do me any good. My eyes can't put up with the brightness. I might even lose my sight altogether for a little while if I spend too much time in the sun. Bright, snowy days like this are the worst. My head starts to ache,' Inkeri explained, trying to keep her voice steady. Bigga-Marja gave her a quizzical look. Inkeri smiled and rummaged in her camera bag for a new roll of film. These last few days she had wondered what type of film to take on the trip, and she was worried she might have made the wrong choice. The film that Bigga was now using required a lot of light, perhaps even more light than was available up here, despite the brightness. Nonetheless, the benefits of that type of film were indisputable: in the development stage, it was possible to enlarge images taken on this film far better than those of other films. This resulted in clearer, less grainy photographs. Inkeri turned the other film in her fingers, the one that didn't need so much light and that she would probably install in the camera once they reached the hotel.

'Do you remember when we talked in class about how light is born?'

Bigga didn't remember.

'It is born in the dark. Light and the sun are one and the same thing. They are both forms of energy, they are fire. *Photograph* really is a smashing word for it. Do you know its original meaning?'

'No.'

'It comes from the Greek, and it means literally drawing with light.'

'*Drawing with light…*' Bigga said, her voice hushed.

'What is it in Sámi?' Inkeri asked eagerly.

'*Čuovgagovva…*' Bigga said quietly after a moment's thought. 'It means *light picture*. Photo, graph. Why can't photographs capture colours too?'

'You know what? They can. I have a special machine that can do just that, but I'm afraid it's broken.'

'Does Melander have a machine like that too?' Bigga asked, and pulled a face. Inkeri chuckled. *Melander*.

'How old is the girl?' Eino Melander had asked her when they were in Helsinki and stared at Bigga's clothes, her Sámi costume, her cap. On the way to the office, Bigga-Marja had been stopped by passers-by at least ten times. As they walked along Bulevardi, someone had even asked to take a photograph of her. Somewhat flustered, Bigga-Marja had agreed and posed for the picture, but later on the whole incident had become a source of great irritation.

'She's nothing but a child,' Melander had exclaimed.

'She's already thirteen!' Inkeri had said in her defence. 'Bigga wants to write a piece for the paper. Just one piece, in her own name and with her own photographs. What harm could it possibly do?'

'Aren't these Sámi folk… How should I put this…? Aren't they lazy and work-shy? About as hard-working as the gypsies, I should say,' Melander scoffed. Inkeri opened her mouth to protest, but nothing came out. 'Does she even go to school?'

'Eino!' she gasped. 'How could you? Of course she goes to school. Everybody has to start somewhere. Bigga has been my assistant for a while now, and I couldn't recommend a better budding reporter. And I believe she should be properly paid, too. Don't you agree?'

Melander looked Inkeri up and down but said nothing. Instead, he reached into a box of paperwork, took out a letter and handed it to her.

'Here. One of your friends brought it.'

'Who?' she asked, though she knew the answer perfectly well.

'How should I know? Red lips and black high heels. Black hair.'

'I see,' said Inkeri with affected nonchalance. She licked her lips. This was why she had wanted to speak to Melander in the first place.

'Well, who is she?' he asked as Inkeri peered inside the envelope.

'An old friend of mine…'

'Has this got something to do with your little operation? Trying to find out what happened to your husband? I had hoped you might have given up by now…' he sighed.

'My friend…' she began. 'She was a double agent who used to work for the Paatsalo Unit.'

'She what?' Melander gasped.

'That's right. The unit carried out reconnaissance activities specifically in the areas of Lapland and Petsamo.'

'Yes, I know that. How do *you* know?'

'Oh, please… In any case, I asked for her help.'

'And she helped you?'

'Yes.'

'Is she passing you information? Isn't that… illegal? More to the point, *why* is she helping you?'

'Imagine this: my friend used to carry a gun in that quaint black handbag of hers. Now all the men have come back from the front and taken her work away, and they expect her suddenly to adapt to life as a dutiful housewife. She's bored to tears.' Inkeri eyed the letter. 'Aha! It says here she has managed to access the documents I asked about… and she's going to send more information about this Saara woman to the reception at the Pallas Hotel, where I shall pick up a delivery in a few weeks' time…' Inkeri cut herself short when she noticed Bigga loitering in the doorway, within earshot. She didn't have the chance to reprimand her, as the girl ran away that very second and sat sulking in the waiting room. 'There, see what you've done now,' she snapped at Melander, as she imagined Bigga must be upset that he wouldn't allow her to work as Inkeri's assistant.

Melander sighed again. 'Very well. Let her be your assistant. I can't very well stop you. And let's agree that if she still wants to be a reporter in a couple of years' time, send her to see me.'

Bigga-Marja was gloomy throughout the journey home, though Inkeri had tried to comfort her and explain that two years isn't all that long. Bigga hadn't said a word about their trip to Helsinki ever since—until now.

'No,' said Inkeri. 'Melander doesn't have a colour camera.'

'Good. That man's an idiot,' said Bigga, and Inkeri laughed. Bigga stopped. They could see movement. The reindeer had come closer, and a bird flew to the ground right in front of them.

'A grouse!' Inkeri gasped. Bigga hunched her shoulders, raised the camera up to her eye and focused the lens.

'As the light is reflecting off the snow, you should use a smaller aperture. Do you remember how to adjust it?' Bigga didn't answer; she was concentrating on taking the photograph. A moment later came the familiar click of the shutter, which frightened the bird away. Inkeri watched as Bigga turned the lever to set the camera up for a new image. The crank wouldn't move. The film had probably come loose from the spool, she thought, but decided to let the girl find out what was wrong and fix it by herself. Bigga-Marja stood up, and they continued on their way.

'When I was still a student at the atelier in Helsinki, the equipment was far more primitive than this. And there was never enough light. The exposure times were so long that we had to tie iron bars to people's backs so they could sit up straight long enough,' said Inkeri, and they laughed.

'If we had been alive a hundred years ago, we would have walked across those fells over there,' Bigga said suddenly, pointing at the row of fells up ahead. 'Actually, even ten years ago, we would have been up there.'

'Have you ever been up there?'

'Yes, when I was a baby, and a bit later too. I spent most of the war in the village with Áddjá, but once or twice I set off with my mother. Uncle Lasse didn't have his farm back then either. Grandpa was the only one in our family who lived in a real house.'

'Do you know the route you took?'

'Some of it. We always left at the beginning of May and headed for Skibotn. The route usually took us through the forests following along the banks of Palojoki, and that led us to the other side of Pallas Fell. Then from there we continued onwards to Karesuando and finally up to the shores of the Arctic Ocean. It always depended on the weather and the condition of the crusted snow wherever we happened to be. And, of course, where the reindeer were.'

'Is that the route that Piera always takes when he goes bootlegging?'

'Maybe. I don't know. But he always visits our clan's *seita* on the way.'

'*Seita*?'

Bigga-Marja watched as Inkeri tilted her head to the side. 'It's a sacred place. He's taken me with him a few times. All the generations before me have visited it too and left sacrificial gifts. All of them, for as long as anybody can remember, for thousands of years. I've visited it by myself too.'

'For thousands of years, well...' Inkeri gave her a sceptical look. Bigga casually shrugged her shoulders.

'How did you get there by yourself?'

'It was easy!'

'Will you show me one day?'

Bigga fell silent.

'Bigga?' Inkeri asked after a moment's pause. She had been waiting for a suitable moment to ask this, but for some reason she'd kept putting it off again and again.

'Yes?'

'What do you know about Olavi?'

Now Bigga stopped still and answered in a flash. 'Why do you want to know?'

'How did he come to live here?'

Bigga's large, gappy front teeth bit into her lower lip, leaving a white blotch in the skin.

'He just turned up one day. I don't know,' she mumbled. The truth was that Bigga-Marja remembered all too well. She remembered the pale man standing on the steps outside the house, looking on in disbelief as her grandfather tried to explain to him what had happened, why everything here was dark and black. She remembered Áddjá telling this strange man that he had arrived too late, but Olavi wouldn't hear a word of it, neither then nor when Bigga-Marja was evacuated with the other children. Later on, nobody was allowed to breathe a word about it. That's what Áddjá had said. And if he said something, it had to be obeyed.

'Why did he come here? And why did he end up living with you? I thought he came here to help build the church, but that can't be true if he'd already arrived before it was burnt down,' said Inkeri. She was unable to gather any more information about Olavi, as they were interrupted by a man in a reindeer-skin coat riding a sleigh.

'*Buorre beaivi*,' he greeted them from afar.

'*Ipmel atti*,' Bigga replied as he brought the sleigh to a halt next to them.

'*Gosa doai leahppi manname? Sáhtángo mun veahkehit?*' asked the man.

Bigga nodded, then turned to Inkeri, who seemed at a loss. 'He's asking if we need any help,' she explained. '*Moai letne manname Bállásii. Bessego du givttas? Moai čálle áviisii. Inkeri lea doaimmaheaddji. Mun veahkehan!*' Bigga chuckled, and proudly showed him the camera.

The man looked at them. '*Gean nieida don leat?*'

'*Mun lean Hágas-Bierá Biggá-Márjá.*'

Inkeri raised an eyebrow; she had never heard Bigga's full Sámi name before. In the school register she was listed simply as Bigga-Marja Iisko.

'*Hágas-Bierá?*' the man asked, his interest now piqued. Bigga nodded with a smirk. There must have been something amusing about this, as the man began laughing too. Inkeri took a deep breath and stared at her shadow. The snow was dappled with black and a golden yellow. Sunspots.

'Get in! He wants to give us a ride!'

'Bigga. *Why* did Olavi come here?' Inkeri asked again. She had to find out. Bigga turned to look at her.

'*Boahttibeahttigo doai?*' the man called, now rather impatient.

'I think he came looking for someone,' Bigga finally admitted.

Inkeri stopped still and turned to Bigga. 'Who was he looking for?' Bigga looked at Inkeri but simply shrugged her shoulders and for the rest of the journey refused to say another word on the matter.

INARI

May 1944

WE SPEND EVERY NIGHT with each other and steal time during the day too whenever we can. Her neck smells of earth and iron, at times it is cold and carries the scent of the wind. Her entire body comes out in goosebumps when I kiss her lower abdomen. I wander along every last fold of skin. There is no surface on her skin that I haven't touched. I know the feel of her earlobe and her fingers against my tongue. I know the taste of her navel.

At first, I always find it hard to look at her properly. Instead I only look at small bits here and there. Her soft, round breasts, her bottom, her thighs, her small toes. Her hard nipples that stand to attention and that she allows me to suckle. When I nibble them, she yowls. How I yearn to capture that sound. That moan means everything to me. Nothing else matters.

At times, simply existing is so hard that it hurts.

May 1944

Fresh snow has fallen, forming drifts across the terrain. White. Grey. Undulating. The ice has cracked here and there, raising its head in the thawed sections of the river. There is only a thin layer of ice left.

I have heard the men say that in southern Germany spring is already so far along that the flowers are in bloom and the birds are singing. Dreams move forwards. Somewhere in the world there are red, yellow, purple, violet and blue flowers that have opened or are about to open. The surrounding greenery protects them.

Here, there is only white, then grey. Sometimes blue. Snow frozen on top of a boulder. Once I caught a glimpse of red. I squinted, tried to focus. Was it blood? I strode nearer to it. It was a willow ptarmigan. Its red markings shone from the fresh snow like an exclamation mark. Its stiff black legs almost at breaking point. A feather frozen in the air.

I crouched down closer to the corpse and looked on in silence. Back in Alakurtti, I once saw an Arctic fox curled up inside a dead reindeer, for protection. Beside it lay an escaped Finnish Spitz. But nothing could fit inside this dead ptarmigan. I had to stand up. The northern sky flared. According to Saara, the Kvens call the aurora borealis the 'Finnmark Fire'. The locals in Inari call it *kuovsâkkâsah*. All I can see is a bloodied mist hanging above the white horizon.

Ash falls from the sky.

May 1944

The runaways have been apprehended. Kalle included. They had been hiding in a cabin with one of the local reindeer herders, who was duly executed. Koskela brought all the prisoners back to the camp.

Right now, one of them is lying on the ground in the kind of position in which most people are born into this world. There is a reddish-brown sludge on his shoes, dripping and staining the snow. I can see someone running towards him, to help him. It's not one of the guards. There is already a guard standing right next to him. This must be one of the prisoner's friends, but he too is shot. It is dark, snow still falling, each flake melting the moment its tiny surface touches the ground.

Heiskanen tries to convince Commander Felde not to execute Kalle. He appeals to Kalle's Finnish roots, points out that technically he's not even a prisoner, that they need him for 'their own operation'.

When I look at the sky, I see white snowflakes falling from the darkness.

ENONTEKIÖ, 1949

INKERI STOOD in the classroom and watched as the pupils drew portraits of the person sitting next to them. She glanced at Bigga-Marja's empty chair and felt anxious. Something had happened. She wasn't entirely sure what, but after their trip Bigga had been even quieter and more irritable than before, just as she was after the excursion to Helsinki. The difference now was that Bigga hadn't attended her classes for a full two weeks. Inkeri had an inkling of why this might be, but she hoped she wouldn't have to bring it up.

Upon arrival at the hotel, Inkeri had left Bigga-Marja taking pictures with the camera and headed straight to the reception desk to ask for the delivery in her name. The parcel was thicker than she had expected. On the top was a letter with familiar handwriting on the envelope. Inkeri knew that her childhood friend had joined the Lotta Svärd Brigade during the war, but from there she had been transferred to an espionage training facility near the Russian border. As the war continued, this friend worked primarily in and around Lapland. At the end of the war, she had contacted Inkeri to tell her she'd found Kaarlo's name in a list of prisoners collated by the Red Cross.

Inkeri leafed through the information that Lotta Niinistö had sent about people of interest. She recalled Melander's words. She didn't know whether her friend had permission to forward such sensitive information, but was it really any of her concern? Inkeri pulled herself together and concentrated on trying to decipher her friend's handwriting. Lotta described Tapani Koskela as an average man. She had seen Inspector Koskela herself on several occasions, and she thought him perfectly affable. What's more, Lotta claimed that, because of his rank, Koskela had probably been granted extensive access to the camps, and it was widely believed that he might in fact have been some kind of liaison officer. Lotta seemed almost certain of this. For this reason, Inkeri should most definitely try to contact him. However, at the time of writing, Koskela was locked up in the penitentiary, so Inkeri would still have to wait a full year until he was released.

She sighed and pushed the papers to one side. On the next pile of papers she saw a familiar name, then glanced quickly over her shoulder to make sure Bigga-Marja wasn't looking. Though Olavi Heiskanen was a relatively common name, Lotta believed she had tracked down the right person. *Olavi Heiskanen: worked on the construction of the military railway at Hyrynsalmi. Discharged in 1942. After this, registered in the Koillismaa District, after which there is no mention of him in any official documentation. His whole family is dead. Father and two brothers killed in action. Mother died in childbirth. Studied theology.*

'Theology?' Inkeri gasped in disbelief, and flicked through the papers in the hope of finding a photograph of the man, but this was everything that Lotta had managed to unearth about him. Inkeri thought it strange: why was there no mention in these documents that Olavi was now working in Enontekiö?

She wondered whether she ought to inform Lotta about this but forgot all about the idea when she picked up the final piece of paper. *Saara Valva.*

If the information on Olavi seemed sketchy, there was even less on Saara Valva. Only a dainty handwritten text: *Place of birth: Russian Empire. Arrived in Finland: 1941. Speaks Finnish fluently, as well as Skolt Sámi, Russian, and several other local languages. Ethnically Sámi from across the eastern border.* And there was a photograph of this Saara. When Inkeri picked up the photograph, she froze. The woman had dark hair and light eyes. Inkeri could feel her heart racing, her skin tingling, and at first she couldn't fathom why. Then it dawned on her that she had seen this woman before. But where…?

She gave a start as Bigga-Marja sat down beside her.

'What are you doing there? You startled me,' Inkeri snapped.

'I've been standing there for a quarter of an hour already, but you didn't notice. I don't like the way those men are looking at me. What's that you're reading so closely?'

'Did you try to interview them?' Inkeri stammered, and quickly stashed the documents in her satchel. At that same moment, she realized that the document about Olavi Heiskanen was still lying right in front of Bigga-Marja's eyes. The girl's mouth looked pinched. Inkeri snatched the paper away, pale as a sheet.

'Did that say Olavi Heiskanen?'

'What?' Inkeri asked. 'Oh, that's nothing… So, did you get an interview with those men?'

Bigga-Marja gave her an indignant look.

'Why are you investigating Ovllá?' she asked.

'We should get going, if we want to get the same ride home,' Inkeri said, and started buttoning up her coat. They then moved towards the front door and walked past a group of men sitting in the reception area. Inkeri concentrated her efforts on examining the men so as not to catch Bigga-Marja's eye. She remembered the men talking loudly about some research they were carrying out; they compared tape measures and wrote down questions. One of the men looked amusing, with bright-red hair and a pair of spectacles. Before long the sleigh arrived, and they left the hotel without saying another word to each other.

Since that day, Bigga-Marja hadn't taken part in any of Inkeri's classes, and Inkeri wondered whether the girl was angry because of her investigation. Olavi, meanwhile, had been behaving normally and hadn't said anything to suggest he knew what Inkeri was up to. It seems Bigga hadn't told him about it after all.

Inkeri snapped out of her thoughts at the sound of raised voices. Niila and Ántte, who by now both spoke good Finnish, and a few of the others were speaking frenziedly, and an argument was about to break out.

'Boys!' said Inkeri, waving her pointer in a show of authority and stepping closer to the children.

'Ántte! How nice to hear that you've learnt our rich national language. But need I remind you, it should be used only for noble purposes. Now, what are you all chattering about?'

'It's nothing, miss...' Niila mumbled.

'Now, now—tell me!'

'It's just that...' Niila glanced up at Inkeri timidly, then looked at the classroom door. Suddenly the room went silent.

Inkeri felt the same as when the boys had been talking about the discovery of the prison camp.

'Well?' she said, her head tilted to one side. 'Stand up when I'm speaking to you!'

'What's happening in the next classroom, miss?' the boy muttered as he stood up.

'What do you mean? Speak loud and clear, please!'

Inkeri surveyed the classroom. Everybody was quiet. Niila looked Inkeri in the eye then lowered his gaze.

'Niila. There's nothing happening next door. What on earth do you think is going on there? School has ended for the day, and there is nobody here but us. My class is the only one held at this time of the afternoon, because this is a voluntary, extra-curricular class.' The sound of muttering buzzed through the room. Inkeri looked around her, then returned her eyes to Niila.

'Very well, then. Let's go and have a look. Niila, you can come with me!'

'But—'

'No buts!' Inkeri exclaimed, and marched out of the room, dragging the boy behind her by the arm. They stepped out into the corridor and stood in front of the door to the adjoining classroom.

'This one?' she asked. Niila nodded silently. Inkeri knocked. There was no answer. Nervously she shifted her weight from one leg to the other and knocked again. This time she heard steps from behind the door. She glanced at Niila; the boy was gripping her arm. As the door opened, Inkeri began explaining in a clipped tone that her student had seemed very interested in what was going on in this room, but the words immediately caught in her throat. The first thing she saw was two men in doctors' coats. Standing right in front of her was the same man she recalled seeing at the hotel in Pallas. He was easy to spot; his red hair made him particularly memorable. Inkeri quickly closed her mouth.

'Ah, Mrs Lindqvist. Would you like to come and watch the measurement? What is young Niila doing with you? He doesn't need to come again. We measured him yesterday.' Speaking to her now was one of the other teachers, a woman whose name she seemed incapable of remembering.

'What measurement?' she asked, and when the other teacher stepped to one side, Inkeri saw a group of five or six children, some in their underpants, some in outdoor clothes, and one standing to the side, naked. She instinctively clasped Niila closer to her. At first, she didn't understand what was going on. She turned her head to look for another teacher but instead she saw Bigga-Marja, her hands clenched into fists, her knuckles white and her eyes fixed on the floor. Though she must have heard Inkeri's arrival, the girl didn't look up; she didn't look at anyone. The classroom was deathly quiet.

'What is going on here?' Inkeri spluttered. For a moment, nobody answered.

'Research,' someone said. Inkeri could see Bigga-Marja's jaw trembling, so single-mindedly was she trying to focus her attention on a single spot on the floor.

Inkeri looked on, paralysed, as one of the men propped his camera in front of the child standing naked. The other man muttered a few numbers, and the red-haired man wrote them down in a notebook. The boy about to be photographed was petrified, his skin covered in goosebumps; Inkeri could see it from the doorway.

'Would you like to stay and watch?' came a voice.

'Excuse me?' Inkeri snapped in disbelief.

'If you have no reason to watch the proceedings, I'm afraid you'll have to leave,' said the voice. Inkeri looked on agog as the redhead raised his eyes and peered up at her with an air of bewilderment, the movement causing the cover of his blue notebook to flap. On the table next to the man was a loose length of measuring tape. Then the door closed in Inkeri's face, and she remained standing in the corridor.

Until now, she had held Niila firmly by the arm. Now she let him go, and he recoiled in a flash. He was pale. So was she.

'Niila,' she said, her voice now steady. 'Go back into the classroom. I'll be there in a moment. Do not talk about this to anybody. Do you understand? Not to anybody!' Niila nodded and slowly walked back into the neighbouring classroom. Once he had shut the door, Inkeri buried her face in her quivering hands.

She didn't know what caused it, but at that moment she suddenly understood why Saara Valva looked so familiar. She was one of the women in the photograph that Inkeri had snatched from the church foundations a few years ago. The woman with the arresting gaze, a look of fear, perhaps, or disgust, an emotion that Inkeri couldn't quite put into words.

INARI

May 1944

THERE ARE RUMOURS that Commander Felde has had an appointment with Saara. I asked her about it. The commander was supposed to depart for Germany today, but his leave has been cancelled. Gossip around the camp says he might have syphilis or gonorrhoea. At first, Saara was reluctant to tell me anything, but eventually she admitted that it was indeed syphilis. In addition, the commander has been put into isolation for two months, just as anyone else would be. Now Felde is unable to take his leave in Germany and he is supposed to abstain from all sexual relations. And on top of this, the doctor gave him a document where he was supposed to write down the name of the woman who gave him the disease in the first place.

'He refused to give them a name,' said Saara, and lit a cigarette. Her name is engraved on the side of her lighter.

May 1944

Without informing the Finnish authorities, the Nazis have begun constructing fortifications across Lapland. Everybody knows what these fortifications will be used for, but nobody dares utter it out loud. Heiskanen expresses his secret concern, but I refuse to discuss the matter with him. Besides, he won't be going to the worksite. We leave in a week.

Another consignment of prisoners arrived yesterday; I don't know where they have come from because Heiskanen is taking care of the interviews. Apart from this shipment, there have been no new prisoners for two weeks. This is because nothing is progressing at the front.

May 1944

At the worksite today I saw a bearberry peeking out from beneath the melting snow. I recognized it from the cover of one of my books. It is a chionophobic plant: it has a fear of snow. Imagine that such plants can exist this far north, plants that are afraid of snow. The bearberry usually thrives on elevated ground whipped by the wind. It is a quirky, captivating plant. *Rievssatmuorji*, Saara taught me to say it in Sámi. I asked how she knows the local language. She told me she speaks five distinct Sámi languages, and on top of those Kven, Norwegian and Finnish. Russian too. And German, of course.

When I tried to ask her more, she didn't answer but smiled and turned away. Saara's smile is the only thing that makes me smile too.

When I touched her back that night it felt cool, but her embrace, that was as warm as the stomach of a cat just woken from its curled slumber.

May 1944

I saw Koskela again today. He has been forced to apply for a new passport. It seems the Nazis have managed to get this demand through—that Finnish policemen now need a new identification card complete with a photograph. There are plans afoot for the rest of us to have such a card too. The Finnish passport process is so chaotic that the Germans will not tolerate it. They require better photographs and more detailed descriptions.

Koskela said that Hillilä, the provincial governor, had eventually acquiesced, though in all other respects he had tried to remain firm, for instance in the debate as to whether Finnish law should continue to apply throughout Lapland. Koskela offered me his hip flask. I doubt its spout has ever been washed; it smelt bad and didn't taste of anything when I took a sip.

All of a sudden, Koskela asked me whether I had noticed any extra transportations and gave me a meaningful look. I went pale. I didn't know what to say. I stammered that I hadn't noticed anything out of the ordinary, though this is not true, and I am sure Koskela realized this. Then I said quietly that I suspect Kalle and Heiskanen have something to do with the matter. I decided not to mention Saara. Koskela nodded, said that it would probably have been best for all concerned if the escaped Finnish prisoner had been found dead. 'That will cause problems yet,' he said pointedly.

May 1944

I asked Saara whether she knew anything about these night-time transportations. She looked at me, amused at first, then asked, perplexed, did I really not know what was going on?

'They're taking prisoners to other camps,' she said.

'What do you mean?' I asked.

'They are being shipped elsewhere to make up numbers in the workforce, sent to Norway or across the border, some even to Enontekiö. All the degenerates are taken to Poland, though there are still a couple of Jews up here at the worksites. In Poland the Jews are carted off to the gas chambers before being incinerated. Like animals,' she said, then turned to face me. 'But you knew that already,' she added, her voice frank and cold.

I told her that's not what I meant.

Saara looked at me long and hard as I tried to rephrase my question. Are they taking bodies elsewhere?

'There are no bodies,' she said, and I instantly regretted asking anything at all, because now I know she is lying to me, and it feels like a thousand knives thrust into my gut. And that was when it hit me, this potent wave of jealousy. Saara and Heiskanen have some kind of pact together. They have a shared secret. Saara places the lighter and her cigarette box back into her pocket and leaves for work. My heart is thumping hysterically.

May 1944

There are over nineteen hours of daylight now. The night is barely five hours long. There is no darkness to speak of.

May 1944

I have been assigned to another camp in the fells. We are beginning work on the fortifications.

ENONTEKIÖ, 1949

A PUBLIC HOUSE HAD BEEN opened next to Kolehmainen's guest house and the village shop, near the church worksite. Outside, it was bitterly cold. The wind howled in gusts, its very sound sending a chill down Olavi's spine. Inside the pub, the air was thick with the customers' breath and sweat. Mixed with the scent of bodies was the aroma of new liquor and tobacco. Piera spun round in his chair to see whether the owner was still watching him, then took a bottle out of his jacket pocket, unscrewed the cap, took a gulp, and handed it to Olavi. With a grimace, Olavi took a swig and gave it back. Piera had returned from the wilderness the day before yesterday. He dug around in his bag and eventually pulled something out.

'Here you go,' he muttered, holding out a pouch made of reindeer skin, sewn together with gut thread and with patterns embroidered in decorative ribbon.

'Thank you.' Glancing inside the package, Olavi recognized the alpine rock cress, the hemiparasitic velvetbells, even the edible mountain sorrel. A sticky substance oozed on to his fingers from the tips of the butterworts. The glacier crowfoots had worked their way to the bottom of the pouch. April had begun. High up in the fells, the reindeer doe had finally started to shed their antlers. The barren doe shed them before the others, as they did not bear calves.

The publican peered at their table.

'What you looking at?' Piera growled. 'Gawking over here like a donkey at a new gate.'

'I've got my eye on you.'

'And why's that?' Piera asked. 'Just having a chinwag with Ovllá here. Minding my own business.'

'But you're not, are you? What have you got in that bag?'

Piera looked up at Olavi and sighed.

'Don't worry. There's no contraband,' said Olavi, and showed him the pouch.

'Flowers?' asked the publican.

'Yes, flowers. From under the snow,' Olavi nodded.

'You're easily amused,' the publican muttered, and walked off to wipe the tables.

'That's all we need, if I get into a jam for these,' Piera chuckled.

'He's probably still fidgety from the shenanigans a few weeks back,' said Olavi. On Annunciation Day, a few of the locals had got into a knife fight with a couple of men from across the border, and not everybody had settled their differences yet.

'Right. Some of these I grew from a cutting in Lasse's greenhouse. Just plant 'em in the flowerbed; maybe next month, once May comes around,' Piera said, and smacked his lips. 'But it'll be short-lived, I tell you. These flowers belong up past the treeline, out on the heath, whipped by the wind. They grow where it's barren. That way their beauty can shine.'

Just then, Inkeri's familiar figure appeared in the doorway. Piera glanced at Olavi and raised his eyebrows.

'Bigga-Marja,' Inkeri stammered. She was breathing heavily. The publican turned to look at the new arrival and seemed to be wondering whether to throw her out or not. A woman couldn't walk into a pub without male company. Piera stood up and raised a hand, indicating that Inkeri was with them.

'Bigga-Marja,' Inkeri swallowed, and tried to steady her breathing. 'She's disappeared.'

'What do you mean, disappeared?' asked Piera.

'It seems she's run away from school.'

Now Olavi stood up too.

'What are you talking about?'

'She's been missing since yesterday.'

'Are you sure?' Olavi interrupted them.

'I'm sure. She's not at school and she's not in the dormitory. I had a look around the house too, but she's not there either. I went to…' Inkeri tried to catch her breath. 'I checked in the shed, and there's a pair of skis missing.'

Inkeri looked at Piera. He glanced first at Olavi, then turned and stared out of the window.

'Since yesterday, you say?' he mumbled. The colour drained from Inkeri's face.

'It's going to be frightfully cold. There's a spring storm coming—it's already twenty degrees below!'

'Yes, it is…' Piera muttered, and walked outside.

'Where are you going?' Inkeri shouted angrily, and followed him. Outside, the pig woke from her slumber and waddled over towards her master.

'I'm going to fetch my skis; I've left 'em up at the house. Olavi, you coming to look for Bigga?'

'Yes, of course,' he said, and the three of them walked off in curious formation back to the house, the pig scuttling beside them.

'Do you think she could pick up Bigga's scent?' Inkeri asked, and looked cautiously at the pig.

'Oh yes. Done all kinds of things, she has. When I was up in the fells looking for missing people and runaways, there's no better tool than a pig's snout.'

'Did you do that during the war?'

'That's where I lost my fingers.'

'What do you mean?' Inkeri gasped. 'I thought a bolt of lightning...'

Piera stopped suddenly and turned to face her.

'What's really going on at that school?' he asked sharply.

'Nothing,' she said defensively, and felt the blood rushing to her cheeks.

'There's something funny going on there, I'll tell you that,' Piera snapped, and continued marching towards the house.

They walked on in silence. Then Piera said: 'Let me tell you what happened here during the war, how I lost my fingers. Can't remember whether it was the 25th or the 26th, but it was November 1944. The Germans had repositioned themselves behind the fortress at Jämärä and stayed there until the following January.'

Inkeri stared at the sky. Stars flickered on the horizon. The moon was bright, dark spots visible on its surface.

'Anyway, I'm used to hiking in the woods, but when there's a war on, things are different. I was starving most of the time. Sure, I killed some reindeer, plenty of 'em, I ate lichen, scavenged for food under the moss, just like the deer, and got myself such stomach pains I thought my time was up. And many's a time I almost got caught. First by the Germans, then by your lot—our own army, which so many of us Lapps had sworn to fight and die for.'

Far away across the horizon was a distant glimmer, like the burgeoning borealis but not quite.

'Don't know why, but the thing I remember most about that time is the flies—screwing one another like there was no tomorrow, they were.'

'In the middle of winter?' Inkeri wondered.

'No… This all happened in the autumn. I don't understand why, but some of the flies hadn't died or hibernated. Still alive, can you believe it? Back then, I still dared start a fire at the tents or huts I stayed in. Every morning I woke to the sound of those damn flies, and there they were, always on top of one another. I heard that buzzing in my ears for a long time after. Still do, sometimes. So…' Piera muttered. 'Tell me, lass, do you know what it feels like to watch your own land burn? They didn't even spare the church. Eventually, they moved up into the fells. I hid out in a hut with a sealed bomb shelter built underneath. I put all the animals down there that I could get my hands on, because I knew the Germans would shoot every last one of 'em as they retreated. I took them to safety, but I let Matilda go free. Don't know why, a sixth sense or something. She just ran off towards the north. And by Jove, can pigs run.' As he spoke, his breath steamed up in front of him. Now he too looked up at the stars. They were already halfway back to the house.

'D'you know the sound of animals being burnt alive?'

Inkeri gulped.

'The fire didn't get into the bomb shelter, but when I finally plucked up the courage to go back there and managed to prise the door open, the creatures were lying all over the place, all swollen up, they were. Everything stank of cooked meat. God, it made me feel sick. Some of the animals had gathered in the middle of the bunker, for safety. Some had struggled for a long time. Some had melted into one another, like tin or cast iron.'

Inkeri heard the crunch of footsteps behind her and ahead of her.

'I didn't dare go anywhere, neither north nor south, east nor west. There were enemies everywhere I looked, destruction all around. It's enough to make you lose your mind,' he said, and came to a halt. 'You mark my words, you'd lose yours too. You of all people.'

'I'm sure,' Inkeri whispered, her cheeks pale.

'There's probably a scientific name for it, but it made me a bit funny in the head. And I'm not ashamed of it neither. I'll freely talk about it,' he said, looking Inkeri right in the eye, then walked off again.

'So there I was, stuck, all alone. The snow was black with soot. It was like the end of the world. The war might as well have continued for another hundred years and I wouldn't have known anything about it. And guess what I heard when I tried to get to sleep at night?'

'The burning animals?' Inkeri's mouth felt dry. They were nearing the house. Olavi had remained quiet throughout the walk. The snow here had melted. The crunch of footsteps had stopped, the sound left behind them.

'Aye, so you'd think. The animals. But no. All I heard was those damned flies screwing one another. And every night I dreamt that my home was on fire and the animals were burning and that the smoke wasn't smoke after all but a swarm of flies. And it suffocated me just like smoke can suffocate animals and humans.'

Inkeri could no longer look at Piera; she couldn't even look in his direction. A cold wind crept in under the hem of her coat. 'One night, I leant a bit too close to the fire. It wasn't on purpose, but it wasn't really an accident neither. It was the first thing in a very long time that actually felt good. You could say I've been burnt now too. At some point, Matilda returned to me, but I don't remember that bit at all. She was frantic, kept nudging me with her snout. If it hadn't been for that pig, I'd have burnt my whole hand, burnt myself alive. In the end, the damage was so bad I had to amputate the fingers. It could've been worse, mind. I haven't missed those fingers once. But I'd have missed living.'

They had arrived at the house. 'Well, it took a while before I realized I couldn't hear 'em any more. The flies,' said Piera. He stopped and turned to look at Inkeri. They had come to a halt by the barn. Piera handed her the pig's leash and picked up his skis, which he had propped against the barn door when he arrived for work in the morning. Olavi disappeared into the granary.

'Bigga-Marja will be fine, even if a storm comes in. You shouldn't worry. When she was evacuated, she got it into her head that Vittangi was somewhere in America. *Are we going to America?* she kept asking over and over,' Piera joked, strapping the skis to his feet. Olavi stepped out of the granary. 'I'll tell you what, though, I've often thought it might as well be just as far. Folk never come back the same.'

Olavi took the flower cuttings from his pocket and handed them to Inkeri.

'Put them in a glass jar and give them some water.'

'I'm coming with you!' Inkeri protested.

'No, you're not,' Piera said in a voice that almost frightened her.

'You stay at the house,' Olavi added in a calmer voice. 'In case Bigga comes back. Now take Matilda indoors. Please, Inkeri.'

'Aren't you taking the pig with you?' Inkeri spluttered.

Piera glared at her. 'I can find her without the pig.'

INARI

May 1944

B UILDING A FORTIFICATION in this weather feels wrong.
It becomes very warm when the sun shines, though there
is still snow on the ground. First of all we built the sauna, and
the prisoners are allowed to use the sauna every day just like the
guards.

Biret-Ánne has joined us on the expedition and is working as a
cook. Right now she has gone off to hunt for a swan. The snow is
so encrusted that she won't leave any tracks. She is a small woman,
and before long she has completely disappeared from view.

Only one prisoner died on the journey. We still don't know
what to do with him, whether to bury him here or take him
back to the camp. The ground is still frozen solid.

But the light—how it draws patterns across the sky. I raise
my bare fingers and see their image etched against the light, and
my sturdy body casts a long shadow across the blanket of snow.

May 1944

Biret-Ánne returned this morning carrying two swans. I heard
the panting of her dog long before I saw the woman herself.

Biret-Ánne was dangling the swans by their necks, then placed them neatly in the sled. She then covered the sled in snow and pushed it into the shade. I don't know what she is planning to do with the swans. Eat them?

At night, I dreamt that Heiskanen and Saara were alone together. They were laughing at me. They went into a farmhouse and locked the door, leaving me out in the cold, alone. When I woke up, I was sticky with sweat.

May 1944

Something miraculous just happened. For the first time, I saw a real convoy of reindeer and traditional herders. You could see them for miles. I'm quite sure they should not be wandering around these parts, but because I was the only one in charge, I allowed them to go on their way in peace, without really knowing why. It soon became apparent that they were heading right through our worksite. Biret-Ánne spoke to them in Inari Sámi and asked where they were going. The herder explained that they were heading to the summer pastures and that this was an ancient route that they had always taken and that they planned to take now. The reindeer bow to the authority of no man.

The sleighs and sleds moved lightly across the crusted snow, though their load was heavy. There was sugar, flour, dried meat, all sorts. The first of the reindeer to approach us looked up at us with large eyes. It was a female and clearly with calf. The animal's instinct was telling it to return to its own birthplace to calve. When it reached us it stopped to eat, scraped at the wet earth, chewed off a piece of lichen visible beneath the snow, and didn't pay us any attention.

When the herders came closer, I heard what sounded like singing. Biret-Ánne told me this was *livde* singing. I had never heard anything like it. I've heard the *yoik*, an ancient form of Sámi chanting, in homes built for the German officers and at dinners where they were served meat and liquor, but on most of those occasions it was only one of the prisoners who was instructed to perform. By now everyone, even the prisoners, had stopped what they were doing, and the guards stood smoking. The black Lapphunds ran up to us and started licking our hands. One of the women had a sling round her neck, her breasts bared so that her baby could suckle as they walked. The prisoners ogled at the woman, and she covered herself up. She took a reindeer antler from the sled, and the baby started suckling on that instead.

A few of the children ran up to the prisoners and began throwing snowballs at them. One small, fair-haired boy didn't have a hat on. He was wearing a black costume made of baize cloth with decorative ribbons in greens and oranges. Strands of hay jutted from inside his shoes.

At first the prisoners didn't react to the children's attempts to play. They were afraid. When they saw that the guards seemed unperturbed, they joined in the game, threw snowballs and started running after one another. This lasted half an hour, maybe longer.

May 1944

We have begun trekking back to the camp. When the sun is shining, it's so hot I have to take my coat off. In weather like this one imagines all kinds of things, perhaps that summer is on its way, though at night the temperature still dips below freezing and we are all afraid of another extended cold spell. That being said, in the thawed sections I can already smell the earth.

The trail of reindeer has gone, taking all the herders with it. Only the prisoners are left, and us. The guards.

May 1944

It is during the quiet moments that it hurts me the most.

When I shut my eyes, I imagine she is next to me. I savour her name, and when I am about to fall asleep I force myself awake, if only to keep the sensation alive.

I close my eyes, and I can feel her soft breast in my mouth, hear the fitful sounds coming from her throat.

At three-thirty, the night is at its most beautiful.

May 1944

Before heading home, Biret-Ánne roasted the swans. The dog struggled beside her, restless and impatient. I stroked the animal. Biret-Ánne said she was waiting for the cur to die.

'Why?' I asked, incredulous, because Biret-Ánne is clearly fond of her dog. Even I understand that.

'It's a herding dog. And there are no reindeer to herd. It's no life, with nothing to do—not even for a dog,' she said.

I watched as she shoved a hand inside the bird and gutted it. The last of the innards to come out was the heart. Finally, she pulled out the swan's windpipe and dried it for two days. She had found a piece of bone somewhere; I don't know whether it was one of the swan's bones. Maybe. Probably. On the final evening, she pressed the bone inside the swan's windpipe, then folded the windpipe into a small round ball that rattled when it moved.

This is a traditional Sámi toy, a cradle-ball, which is reputed to keep evil spirits at bay. They are often given to newborn babies. Local legend has it that the swan-bone rattle makes wings grow from the child's feet.

So, at a moment of peril, it can fly to safety.

ENONTEKIÖ, 1949

O LAVI GAZED OUT towards the lake through the falling snowflakes. It was cloudy, and the stars were momentarily hidden from view. A small flurry of snow was driving in across the lake. It had been three days since she had gone missing, and Bigga-Marja was lying, dozy and feverish, at her Uncle Lasse's new house, which he had built with the money they were given for the evacuation. Inkeri was indoors. Bigga had wanted Inkeri to show her the new camera she had ordered from the Continent. Olavi had followed Inkeri into the house to see if there was anything he could do. There wasn't. Of course there wasn't.

'It's happened before, mind, back in 1920. Kajava sent his quacks up here to measure our skulls. Stripped us all naked, they did, and took pictures from the front and the back. They even photographed our eyeballs, dug up the graves on Inarinsaari and took the skulls away.' Piera spat on the ground. 'Seems the bastards are back.'

Olavi was thinking about the spring, the summer.

'In this frozen weather, it's hard to imagine that it's warm somewhere else,' he said. 'That somewhere far away it's dry and there are palm trees, flowers grow night and day, regardless of the season, the sun rises and sets at exactly the same time every day and the trees twist in different directions than they do here.'

Piera gave him a puzzled look.

'Do you ever think about things like that?' asked Olavi.

'Like what?'

'That somewhere there are palm trees.'

'No, I don't think about that. Ever.'

'You don't wonder what it would be like somewhere else?'

Piera paused for a moment and pondered.

'If I'd spent my whole life right here in this village, I might say if you don't know about other places, you can't miss 'em. But you can't really say that either, now, can you? I've seen a fair bit of the world in my day. But I was made for these parts, that's just the man I am. Put it this way, whenever I'm away from home, I think about what I have back here. But when I'm here, I don't think about what exists someplace else.'

'Home sweet home.'

'Mind you, if you ask me, travel might be the most important thing in the world,' said Piera. Just then the door opened. Inkeri peered outside and stepped into the yard.

'What do you know about travel?' she asked, somewhat surprised.

'Well… When you walk up and down these fells long enough, you get some idea of it,' Piera replied, and looked up at the sky. Olavi threw his cigarette to the ground and lit another one. The ember crackled in the frozen air. Lanterns hung from the doorframe. The Great Bear had appeared, suspended in the northern sky almost directly above them. The constellation had moved slightly from where it had been earlier that evening.

Everything in the sky moved in relation to the North Star. Such things showed the passing of time, demonstrated that time had not stopped, that there was still something shifting and living, always moving forwards.

'Why did the lass go running off like that?' asked Piera, his voice choked. 'She's within an inch of her life.'

'She's all right now. The doctor said she's been in good shape all the while,' Inkeri reproached him.

'Did she say anything to you?' Piera asked her. 'About why she ran away?'

'No…' Inkeri mumbled, trying to avoid eye contact.

'Really? Well, she told me she'd seen some men in suits up at the Pallas Hotel.'

'What about them?' said Inkeri defensively.

'It's just I heard talk these men paid a visit to the school too. Research, they called it.' Piera and Inkeri stared at each other for a moment. Inkeri rolled her eyes.

'Olavi,' she said frostily. 'I came to say that Lasse will get the horse ready, then we can all go home.' She glanced at Piera. 'I'll go and say goodbye to Bigga. I've given her my old camera, so that once she recovers she can take pictures of the landscape.' Inkeri stepped back indoors, closed the door behind her. The dull thud echoed through the night.

'Did the lass say anything when you found her?' Piera asked Olavi. Olavi looked at him. After a few kilometres of searching, the men had split up. There were two ways to reach Lasse's cottage. Olavi had taken one of them and Piera the other. After skiing for three hours, Olavi had finally spotted a small campfire. He remained about fifty metres away and watched. He took out a cigarette, lit it and smoked it in peace. For some reason, he needed to think what to do. Should he approach Bigga or let her be? Should he turn back and claim he hadn't seen her? He didn't know where the thought had come from. It felt so silly, so mindless—to leave a helpless young girl out here in the cold night right where he found her. Perhaps he had imagined that sooner or later she would find her own way home. And if she didn't, someone else would find her. Olavi's cigarette hissed as he dropped it on to the snow. He sighed, aware of the possibility that she might never find her way home, then he picked up his ski poles and quietly pushed himself towards the fire.

He found Bigga-Marja huddling miserably on the ground; she had made a fire, but not much else. She must have heard the whoosh of Olavi's reindeer-hide skis, but she remained utterly motionless. Olavi whistled quietly. He took off his skis and placed his rucksack on the ground, then moved closer when he heard Bigga whistling back—almost imperceptibly, but there it was, all the same. The crusted snow crunched. The makeshift campfire crackled, green and orange soot raining down on the surrounding snow, flakes of ash floating here and there, a charred stump of wood. Further off, the ice cleft across the lake.

Despite the wind, Bigga's tangle of fair hair was jutting in all directions at once. Olavi placed a hand on the girl's head and stroked her hair. 'Quite a trick you pulled there.' He took off his coat, making the smell of sweat puff into the air, and wrapped it round the girl. 'You're frozen stiff.'

'I don't want to go back there.' Tears and mucus had trickled into her mouth, and Olavi wiped her face with his sleeve.

'Where?'

'School.'

'What's happened?' Olavi asked, and stood next to her. She gave off a pungent odour, fresh and wild. It smelt new and raw.

'Some men turned up at school,' Bigga muttered, stoking the fire with a branch. 'I saw them up at Pallas, sitting around in their fancy clothes, their dark suits, brimmed hats propped on their knee. They were pale as the snow.'

'Who were they?'

Bigga-Marja shrugged. Olavi sat down in the snow next to her. One of his skis began sliding down the hill, but he managed to snatch it before it slipped out of reach.

'They were taking photographs,' she blurted out. 'Why were they taking pictures, Ovllá?' Bigga raised her head and looked him in the eye. 'What will they use those pictures for? That's what I've been trying to think about. I would never use pictures like that anywhere.' Bigga's final word cracked as she burst into sobs.

Olavi knew what pictures like that were used for. At the camps, they had measured the inmates' height, their bellies, everything imaginable, and the information was logged in a ledger. He thought of all the countless measurements he had taken. Charts and graphs then showed which race each person belonged to, who was one of the Finnic peoples, who was Russian, who belonged to the Äyrämöinen or Komi tribes. He learnt why it was important to sterilize people or give them certain medications. Once the medication had been administered, he had to observe how the prisoner reacted, how they died and why. And once the prisoner was dead, he had to conduct a detailed autopsy to establish the cause of death. Olavi sighed and looked at Bigga, who had now started hitting the branch against a larger log. It was so strange that some things continued just as they had before, though the war had ended long ago. Strangest of all was that life had carried on, despite the war.

They remained sitting there, listening to the crackling. When the fire began to die down, Bigga-Marja slumbered against Olavi's side. An hour passed, two perhaps. Maybe it was only half an hour. Sometimes time disappeared like that. At some point, Olavi woke her. They put out the fire, strapped on their skis and headed east. They skied in silence, only a hint of sorrow betraying the other's presence.

Olavi awoke from his thoughts when Piera sighed and spluttered, clearing his throat.

'From the moment Inkeri came here, that lass has followed her around like a seagull after a fishing boat,' he said.

'That's not necessarily a bad thing.'

'I'm not sure Inkeri's little hobbies are good for a girl like that. We used to be able to teach our children about our own way of life, how to live in the fells and hunt for food, to take only what you need and no more; how to see where the fowl have made their nests if you wanted to hunt them. And we didn't hunt 'em for fun, mind. Grouse, sometimes, but never a ptarmigan.' Piera lit his pipe. 'But these kids born after the war will never learn things like that. They'll never learn not to hunt the ptarmigan.'

Olavi pulled out his hip flask and took a swig, then handed it to Piera. The old man carried on talking. He asked Olavi whether he knew that, like all the other Sámi men, his youngest son Oula—Bigga's father—had begun his military service up in Petsamo. They wanted all the Sámi men to fight at the front in the north. They were better than the Finns at negotiating the local terrain, they knew how to hunt in the wild, and could tell just by looking at the sky where was north and where was east—the direction in which they were ordered to advance. Oula was eventually sent to the front at Salla; he crossed the border, and from there he headed to Kiestinki. Straight into hell. Nobody came out of that battle alive. Not even those who returned.

'One time, when the boy was here on leave, he complained about how hard everything was. There was so much forest in the east that you couldn't feel the wind. The sky curved in a funny way, and it was dark in the summer. Oula felt as though he couldn't breathe down there, thought the feeling was killing him. But in the end it was a simple little bullet that took him.' Piera said he would never forget how, on his final leave before he died, Oula came home and headed straight up into the fells, sang the old *yoiks*, came back down and left, and never returned again.

'How can something that doesn't even exist control your whole life like that?' asked Piera. Olavi didn't know. He stared at the ground. Piera finished his smoke; Olavi too. For a moment they looked at the stars.

'The Great Bear.'

'The Plough.'

'Cassiopeia.'

'We call it *Sarvva*, the Great Elk, that one there,' Piera said, pointing up at the sky. 'It's guarded by Riibmagállis, the greatest and most powerful of the *stállu* spirits. Those ones over there are trying to shoot the Great Elk,' he said. They stood in silence. Eventually Olavi turned his head.

'Be that as it may, you know fine well none of this is Inkeri's fault,' he said pointedly.

Piera looked at him. 'I know. But I can't help feeling as though I'm losing that lass altogether.'

INARI

May 1944

W<small>E HAVE ARRIVED</small> back at the camp. The prisoners who died on the expedition were buried this evening. Six in total.

My hands are quivering as I walk towards the doctor's cabin, but he's not here today, and I can't go into the village at this hour; besides, I don't have permission to leave the camp. I will simply have to grin and bear it, to wait and endure.

Midnight is nothing but light.

May–June 1944

The melting snow has caused some local flooding. Water levels in the lake have risen, too, and have now reached the graves, bringing bodies to the surface. The smell hangs everywhere, attracting scavengers to the camp; the dogs are barking day and night. The reindeer keep well away. We will have to come up with something, clear some ground and build a new burial site, but the prisoners are reluctant to move the bodies. Many of the prisoners have come down with an upset stomach, and they suspect the bodies are spreading disease. They might well be right.

At night, I hold the cradle-ball in my fingers and don't know what to think. I still haven't seen Saara, and she hasn't left me any kind of message. I've already wondered whether or not I imagined the whole thing. What if she never comes back? The thought nags away at me. I can feel the fear of it at the bottom of my stomach and I cannot eat. Heiskanen seems to have disappeared too. Are he and Saara in the same place?

Some of the bodies have started to saponify, a grey, waxy substance forming across their surface.

June 1944

I dream that Saara and Heiskanen are lying in bed together, sweaty and spent, in the borderland between pleasure and consciousness. Everything smells of the lust that has erupted between them. Saara gently bites Heiskanen's earlobe, then nibbles at his member with her front teeth and soft tongue.

June 1944

I haven't slept for many nights. The nightmares keep me awake. During the day, I try to focus on my work. There is a shortage of food. I've just completed another order. For the trusted prisoners, I have ordered an extra 100g of bread and sugar. I decided that everyone will get the same amount of potatoes; half will go to the prisoners.

In the summer light everything looks different. It is strange to think that this is the same place as it was during the winter. When it is light, you realize how great and strong the darkness really is. You can get used to it at any time of year, the fact that there is no light at all, only darkness.

June 1944

Once again leaflets have been delivered to the camps about the results of research into the creation of a pure Aryan race. The texts are intended to raise morale, especially at a time like this. The guards were passing one of these leaflets around. Dr Mengele has succeeded in creating a perfectly blue-eyed child by injecting a chemical substance directly into a child's eyes.

At this very minute, a dozen or so Jewish eyeballs are preserved in glass jars and stored in a small white vitrine at the Kaiser Wilhelm Institute. The eyes are surrounded by a haze of small, translucent blood vessels, like the filament of roots on a plant cutting.

June 1944

There is an infectious disease spreading through the camp, possibly airborne. Who knows? Those who are infected become terribly weak, guards and prisoners alike.

The day before yesterday saw a number of partisan attacks

closer to the border, but on the Finnish side. The Soviets attacked a few camps and let any Russian prisoners free. All the guards were executed.

Heiskanen has returned to the camp.

ENONTEKIÖ, 1949

INKERI SAT IN HER CAR outside the police station in Rovaniemi and checked herself in the mirror. She had taken off her new round sunglasses that she had ordered, smuggled from America. She looked at the town around her. It had become busier, and more buildings had been constructed since the last time she had visited. That was years ago. Now everything felt as though it had happened years ago. The journey had been dreadful, utterly unbearable. How could she forget how miserable it was travelling along these roads?

The ground had thawed. Small buds could be seen in the trees. It was May. Rovaniemi was so far south that when she opened the car door, the earth smelt the way it should at this time of year. When summer finally arrived, it came quickly. The brightness knocked people off-kilter. If you weren't careful, it could blind you.

Inkeri tidied some errant locks of hair using a clip with the silhouette of a dragonfly etched into its side. She stepped out of the car and saw Tapani Koskela in the distance, then closed the door without locking it. Her hair bobbed up and down as she walked. It was heavy and felt as though it was always in the way. She needed a proper cut, a proper shaping. While she was in Sweden, Inkeri had had it cut stylishly short and donated her hair to charity. In her hair's lifespan, that was fifteen centimetres ago. In that time everything had changed. Nations had been destroyed, new ones established in their place, and within the new borders people tried to survive from one day to the next. Life was full of setbacks, and though there were brief moments of happiness, they too felt leaden.

'A penny for your thoughts,' Inkeri said quietly as she approached the man. Koskela turned to face her. He smiled, lowered his binoculars.

'I'd be a poor man.' His voice and tone were much softer than on the telephone. Inkeri hadn't expected this, and she was slightly taken aback. On one occasion he had even hung up on her.

'You're so hard to track down, I was beginning to think you must be dead.'

The man turned back to face the bright yellow sun.

'I've been busy,' he continued jovially and smiled.

'I can imagine,' Inkeri conceded. 'Eight years in the penitentiary. It's a long time.'

'Certainly is,' he nodded.

'Early release?'

'That's right.'

'Inkeri Lindqvist,' she introduced herself, and proffered her hand.

'Tapani Koskela.'

'Care for a cigarette?' she asked, and Koskela nodded. Inkeri held out her cigarette box. 'There are a few I've rolled myself, but the rest should be factory-standard. Just an old habit of mine,' she said, looking him in the eye with a smirk. Tapani Koskela lit his own cigarette first, then leant over to light hers.

They took their first puffs in silence. Birds tugged dried leaves out from beneath the snow.

'What are you looking for?' she asked.

'The migratory birds. Right now, all I can see are the resident species.'

'For some reason, I've never particularly cared for spring.'

'Is that so? I find it a splendid time of year. The birds return, the snow melts. Day is longer than night. The midges don't bite, and there's no overnight frost. Not very often, at least.'

'Really? Now, I believe you have some information that I need.'

'So you say, but I don't think I can be of much use to you.'

'I beg to differ.'

'I'm a tired old man.'

'And I'm a tired old woman,' Inkeri muttered. 'Kaarlo Lindqvist,' she said, her voice now firmer, and handed him a photograph of her husband. Koskela examined the photograph. Inkeri examined Koskela. He had a round face, and his eyes looked cheerful. He was fair-haired and perhaps a little over-weight, though his time in prison had doubtless slimmed him down. Some people seemed naturally chubby. The colour of the police cap suited his eyes. Koskela took a quick drag on his cigarette, but nothing suggested that he recognized the man in the photograph.

'These are things we're not allowed to speak about, even if we want to.'

'Do you know anything about him?'

Tapani Koskela fell silent.

'You are the only person I can ask. Everyone else refuses to talk.'

'I have no desire to go back to prison,' said Koskela. He leant against the beam of the light wooden terrace and folded his arms.

'What were you charged with?'

'I was on the losing side of the war. And now I've been assigned to work at the vice department,' said Koskela. 'I don't know whether to laugh or cry. Once upon a time, I said I'd rather eat horse dung than end up working there. But here I am. And there's plenty of work. You're a reporter, I take it?'

Inkeri nodded.

'You should write a story about how the Finnish employment office traded girls across Lapland throughout the war. Young girls, most of them completely unaware of what was in store for them.'

'And what *was* in store for them?' Inkeri asked.

'They became servant girls for the Nazis. And in practice, of course, that meant...' Koskela began, but left the sentence hanging. Inkeri blushed.

'How many girls I must have sent to the labour camps... In a war like that, you'd think people would have better things to do,' he sighed. Inkeri blinked.

'Well, shall we go indoors?' Koskela suggested, and opened the door of the police station. The building was empty. Koskela sat down at his desk. His bear-like figure made him look soft and trustworthy. Inkeri found it hard to imagine that he had been involved in murders and executions or that he had worked as a double agent.

'You were seen in Enontekiö around the time when my husband was registered at the camp there and disappeared,' Inkeri began.

'And?'

'I thought that—'

'What did you think?'

'You know what I thought.'

Koskela's expression gave nothing away. Inkeri placed Saara's photograph on the table, the one she had received from Lotta Niinistö.

'Do you know this woman? Perhaps you interviewed her?'

Without even looking at the picture, he said: 'Tell me how you found out about your husband?'

Inkeri shifted position in her chair but didn't reply.

'Those who were allowed to send letters were forbidden from contacting people outside the occupied territories. And according to my information, you were in Sweden at the time. Sweden was outside the occupied territories.'

Inkeri looked at the inspector and explained.

'But how did you know to look for your husband's name in the list of prisoners?'

'Well, I know that the prisoner lists the Nazis handed over to the Red Cross are incomplete, but—'

'How did you know to look for his name there of all places?' Koskela pressed her. His expression had changed now. It was no longer soft and benign.

'An old acquaintance of mine used to work for the Paatsalo Unit. She happened across the name on the list and…' Inkeri mumbled, not knowing quite how to continue. Koskela observed her in the same way he did the birds.

'But have you ever wondered *why* this contact wanted to help you? Don't you find it at all suspicious?' he asked, and picked up the picture from the table. 'This woman's name is Saara

Valva. As to her whereabouts right now, I have no idea. The last time I saw her was in Enontekiö. I'm afraid I don't know anything about your husband.'

'I have come here all the way from Enontekiö. No, in fact I've come all the way from Sweden to get to the bottom of what happened to my husband,' she said, trying hard to keep her voice steady. 'I need information.'

Koskela took out his pipe and began filling it with tobacco. The aroma was different from her own tobacco. Perhaps he smoked it specifically for the fragrance, she wondered.

'Einsatzkommando Finnland,' Koskela sighed, and rubbed his face, took off his peaked cap. His fringe was damp with sweat. 'That's what they called it. It has a longer, more complicated name too, but let's go with this one.'

Inkeri brushed a few static hairs from across her face and began fumbling in her bag for a pen and paper, but Koskela raised a hand.

'No. This conversation is strictly unofficial, and there must be no record of it at all. Do you understand?' Inkeri lowered her hand and pushed the half-visible notebook back into her bag.

'Einsatzkommando Finnland was a Nazi paramilitary unit operating under the auspices of the Security Police, and the Finnish state helped them to procure interpreters for the camps. Every interpreter was accompanied by a Finnish police officer.'

'Very well.'

'The unit's function was quite simply to find and identify ideological and racial enemies.'

'What happened to the prisoners?'

'We were ordered to kill them,' Koskela replied bluntly.

Inkeri's mouth felt dry. 'And you were at a camp like this?' she asked, her voice barely audible.

'Yes.'

'Is that why you were in prison?'

Koskela laughed. 'Yes, *that's* why,' he quipped. 'The unit operated at the Stalag camps in Salla and along the eastern frontier, camps number 309 and 322. It was eventually disbanded in 1942.'

'But?'

'There are no buts,' he smiled. Inkeri had picked up her pen and began tapping it against the surface of the table, the way she always did when she was nervous.

'Except…' he began. Inkeri stopped tapping the pen. 'Some of the officers and interpreters were subsequently transferred to similar duties at other camps.'

'Such as the camp in Inari?' Inkeri asked, and sat up in her chair.

'Yes.'

Inkeri could feel her nostrils flaring.

'I don't know what happened to your husband Kaarlo Lindqvist,' said Koskela after a short pause. 'And I have no intention of going back to prison. You must appreciate, there was a war going on… It's all about perspective. If things had turned out differently, those mistakes wouldn't have been considered mistakes after all.'

'Oh, I see, you were all just victims of circumstance?' she scoffed in angry frustration. 'Couldn't you think for yourselves?'

'People are not built to think for themselves, Mrs Lindqvist,' said Koskela, suddenly steely and formal. 'People *think* they are radical, but their ideas are rarely in any way unique. Even Hitler wasn't unique in his thoughts, and he wasn't especially competent either. He had a stroke of luck. People are lazy that way. They might imagine they can think for themselves and live a truly exceptional life—gallivanting around Africa taking photographs, for instance—but is that really thinking for themselves?' said Koskela, then added: 'I understand you're a keen photographer?'

Inkeri nodded, pale. She had placed her hands in her lap. They were clammy with sweat.

'Then you surely know all about the art of illusion. Even the best of us can be deceived by illusions.'

Inkeri's heart was thumping in her chest. She could barely breathe. The wind whipped outside; birds flew back and forth. She recalled Piera's words. *The birds have lost their minds.*

'War is very similar. The real war is being fought somewhere far away from the front line. The real war is something altogether different,' he said, his voice serious, then fell silent. Inkeri stared at the edge of the table.

'I didn't mean… I…' Inkeri swallowed. 'I know all this. But do you understand, I have nothing left. Finding out what happened to him is all that matters to me now.'

Koskela stared contemplatively out of the window.

'The person who mentioned Saara Valva to you was right: she would certainly know a thing or two about what happened. I'm afraid I don't have the faintest idea where Miss Valva is hiding at present. There is a warrant out for her arrest, so if you ever do come across her, I would very much like you to inform me about it too.'

Inkeri desperately tried to think what other information she might be able to drag out of Koskela, then asked: 'What was the name of the interpreter you worked with at the camp?'

'That was Väinö. Väinö Remes,' he replied. Inkeri looked out of the window.

'Do you think this Väinö knew Saara?'

Koskela let out a dry laugh; Inkeri turned her head and looked at him quizzically.

'Oh, yes. He knew her all right,' Koskela replied.

INARI

June 1944

S AARA has returned.

June 1944

Saara came to me straight away and apologized for having been unable to get here sooner. 'Too much work,' she said, and explained that she'd had to travel up to Parkkina. I don't know what to think. Is she avoiding me?

We spent the night at her lodgings in the parish village, and on the way there I saw Koskela. According to him, she is telling the truth. He was in Parkkina too, where he and Saara took care of some matters at the district court. Foetal terminations and the like.

June 1944

This morning, Saara had a surprise for me. She had kept quiet about it until then. She was excited to show me a small flowerpot with a seedling in it. It was a Lappish rhododendron!

'Where did you get this?' I asked, genuinely bewildered. This is a rare plant, and I have read that its blossom is a thing of exceptional beauty. I cannot wait for it to flower.

'One of the privates brought the cutting with him from Utsjoki, and I decided to buy it for you as a gift. How do you like it?' she said in that affectionate voice that she uses only rarely.

I said I thought this plant only grew in western Lapland, and that if it had been discovered somewhere else, we should report it to the botanical institute at the university. Saara laughed, asking whether I had suddenly become a botanist. No, I chuckled, and told her that I research culture. That's what I studied at the university. That and languages, until the war broke out and I was forced to return to Koillismaa, where I was eventually conscripted.

I keep this flower near me at all times. I shall wait for it to grow, my eyes peeled. Nobody has ever given me anything this beautiful, anything that was so specifically meant for me.

June 1944

We cannot sleep at all. There is nothing but light. The birds sing all through the night. Overnight, small buds have appeared on the rhododendron in its flowerpot, and you can just make out their burgeoning colour. I tell Saara that her eyes are the same colour as the flowers. She laughs and looks away, blushing slightly. She lies down next to me, sniffs the sweat of my armpits, runs her tongue through my body hair and tastes me all over until her cheeks are red, but not from shame. She puts her lips to my ear and whispers my name.

June 1944

It has been a clammy day, then there came a thunderstorm. I saw a bolt of lightning too. The flower's buds contract and open again in the electrified air. Rain batters against the sides of the weapons and the shovels, but we continue working, paying no heed to the storm.

It seems that Commander Felde has got one of the local Lappish girls pregnant, and now he is trying to acquire a marriage licence. He is writing a letter to Hitler himself. The man has lost his mind. Heiskanen looked me right in the eye and joked that soon it might be my turn to write Hitler a letter too. This is the first thing he has said to me voluntarily in weeks, and I could have punched him square on his filthy mouth.

June 1944

Repairs to the roads continue apace. Even the prisoners are wondering out loud why this renovation work is suddenly so important. We repair the broken asphalt. The old material must first be loosened with a pickaxe, then we melt it down and use it to resurface the road afresh. The prisoners dig up the road with their bare hands, working around the clock. This week's theatre group has been cancelled too, which has had a clear impact on morale.

Yesterday we caught a glimpse of the glowing green light that can only be seen at these latitudes. You see it when the sun appears to be setting, then suddenly starts rising again.

June 1944

Koskela visited the camp today. He was here in an official capacity, paid a visit to the command, then stayed behind and had a drink with me. We smoked and spent an hour talking about nothing in particular, the construction of the road and how everything needs to be ready before winter sets in again. He seemed on edge, told me all kinds of things. Apparently, the mood in the village is fractious, they are calling it a summer of fear. The war effort is not progressing the way it should.

Perhaps this is why he pulled me close and told me everything he knew. He said he knows about the bodies that have been transferred to the University of Helsinki for examination, that it isn't legal, and that the government is looking into the matter.

That I should be careful.

That none of this will end well.

He saw my puzzled expression.

'You mean you don't know?' he asked, and lowered his head. Then he explained that the bodies are first surveyed here at the camp, then sent to a laboratory where their racial features are examined in greater detail in order better to understand the coming eugenics programme and to ensure the continued purity of the Finnish race.

June 1944

I have ordered more potatoes. Food provisions are running low. I haven't seen Saara. Perhaps this is for the best. I am still thinking about Koskela's story. I must find out whether it is true or not.

More prisoners have arrived. At first, I wondered whether they had been transferred from other camps, but then I saw their expressions. The older prisoners don't have that look about them. These ones still have a glimmer of hope and fear in their eyes.

June 1944

Last night some of the prisoners were transported away. The living and the dead.

June 1944

Heiskanen and I go through the new arrivals.

I tell him I know about the operation. He says nothing. He looks neither surprised nor frightened. His face is blank.

I ask why Kaarlo is here.

'You realize there is a group of people even lower than the Jews?'

I did not know this.

'They are the most degenerate element there is, barely human, stuck at the anal stage of development. Deformed, effeminate creatures,' he said, and puffed on his cigarette. 'At the front, the men look the other way. When you can't get the real thing, you make do with what's available. In the German camps, these miscreants wear a pink triangle, and they will even kill a Jewish prisoner just to secure a better position in the hierarchy.' There was a hint of frustration in his voice, and something else too. Panic, perhaps, or disgust. Panic.

'When they arrested Kalle before he was brought here, they caught him in the act with another fugitive. Normally, that would have meant a bullet in the head; but he is Finnish. So they brought him here, and we received orders to execute him. But he and I made a deal. Kaarlo puts his name on all official documentation. If something comes up in the future, something that won't stand the light of day, he is responsible for everything.'

I don't say a word.

'Saara helps out with all this. Everything goes past her.'

June 1944

Just now, I saw an encounter between two pairs of birds right at the zenith of the ice-blue sky. They flew towards each other, and at first it looked as though they had collided, but then they continued in different directions. I wondered whether the couples were the same, had they swapped partner in mid-air, and if they had, how would we know? Would they even know it themselves?

III

INARI

S AARA IS WORKING TODAY. I saw her talking to Heiskanen. I was on my way to the barn, and a moment later she followed me in there and looked at me cautiously, as if to apologize for something. She approached me, closed the door behind her, just as she had done the first time we met there. She tried to kiss me, but I turned my head away, then she struck me square in the face, opened her shirt buttons and offered herself to me. Of course I couldn't help myself, I became hard straight away, and she knew it. She pushed me back on to a stool and climbed on top of me, her eyes fixed on me all the while. It didn't last long. She didn't make a sound. She waited for me to turn flaccid, and when I eventually slipped out of her she stood up, leaving in my arms a heavy, ghostly emptiness.

June 1944

When we saw each other today, just the two of us, we were ready to talk.

I told Saara that I knew about Kalle. And the operation.

That it is a dangerous path. I asked how she could bring herself to do something like that.

'We don't have many options. Any of us,' she said under her breath. 'I don't want to end up a whore like so many before me. This isn't what I believe or what I want. But I believe in survival.'

At first we spoke only a little, then curled up in bed together; but something was different now. She raised her eyes, her head resting on my chest, and I could see that she was thinking very carefully about what to say next.

'Another consignment of prisoners is leaving tomorrow,' I said.

'Transportation of living prisoners is a good way to move bodies without anybody noticing,' she said, and after that we lay in silence. We could do nothing else. This is the way things are. If only everything were different, but it is not.

After a few hours, she finally drifted off to sleep, though she had been pretending to sleep all the while. I noticed it from the way she started grinding her teeth, her head resting against my chest.

June 1944

Now I understand why Felde wants to get rid of Heiskanen. Now I understand why I am here. The war has started to turn against us. He wants to get rid of everything that might cause him problems. And because Heiskanen is Finnish, it's not all that easy to get rid of him.

That's why Felde has asked me to spy on him.

June 1944

I have been having difficulty concentrating on anything. Saara too has been listless. Last night she asked me to touch her in a way that I have never touched her before. After this, she climbed on top of me and gyrated like a snake. I don't know where she has learnt all this. I daren't ask.

I dream that, for the first time, I get a good look at all the hearts, eyes, kidneys and livers preserved in bottles in Saara's room. I see her sewing up the skull with a long, sturdy needle. I see her as she wrenches out the heart, sniffs it, deems it rotten and throws it away.

June 1944

I have been unwell. Heiskanen has been ill too. It seems we have all caught this disease. I have difficulty breathing. My heart is racing. I am sweating profusely. I feel hot, then suddenly cold again. They have prescribed a drug that is supposed to soothe me.

What if I simply disappear at this camp, I wonder. What if nobody remembers who I am? Only I will know that I ever existed.

I flinch at every footstep, every bump. Even at the theatre group I am on edge; I don't really know why. I cannot bear to see Kalle. I cannot bear to see Heiskanen either. I've asked to be transferred to other duties. Felde looked at me, his brow furrowed. To him too I am nothing but a marionette.

As I sleep, I can hear prisoners being taken away, the sound of Saara and Heiskanen talking to each other. They lock the door. They are talking about me. Of that I am absolutely certain. They are colluding together. They are together.

Well, perhaps. This fever and the eternal light are playing with my mind.

June 1944

Saara is being sent to Varangerfjord in the occupied zone. I don't know how long she will be away. I have nightmares. I'm worried that she might never come back. She is nervously flicking her lighter. When I ask how she is doing, she doesn't answer.

June 1944

Some of the prisoners have become very ill, bent double with diarrhoea and stomach cramps. One of them, a young Eastern European man, has expelled his own bowels. That was ten days ago.

He still hasn't died.

June 1944

The rhododendron is in bloom.

ENONTEKIÖ, 1950

'*THIS IS THE MESSAGE of good deeds, the message that men can find each other in spite of war, in spite of differences in race.*' Inkeri read aloud a section of text taped to the school bulletin board. It was an extract from the speech the Quakers had given a few years earlier when they were awarded the Nobel Peace Prize. Because it mentioned Finland, this copy of the speech still hadn't been taken down, though the Quakers had all long since gone home. In fact, it was strange that in her three years at the school Inkeri hadn't noticed the speech until now. She took a sip of coffee and placed her cup on its saucer. The school had won a national drawing competition, or rather one of the pupils had won, and Inkeri wished to celebrate the event with coffee and cake and turn it into a real occasion for the whole village. She could sense the atmosphere, and walked up to Bigga-Marja, Piera and Olavi.

'Hello, Bigga-Marja.'

'It's Marja,' she snapped with a toss of the head.

'Bigga-Marja,' Inkeri repeated.

'Who are you to decide what my name is? From now on, it's just Marja, and that's the end of it.'

Olavi and Piera watched the bickering from afar. Inkeri and Bigga had begun arguing more frequently. According to

Inkeri, their photoshoots had become all but impossible, and Bigga rarely wanted to take part in them any more. After one of their rows, Bigga had used the wrong kind of film for the setting, allowing too much exposure, which led to the film burning through and snapping. Inkeri was certain the girl had done this on purpose. Bigga complained that Inkeri couldn't stand even the slightest mistakes.

'Lord, are you still going on about that...?' Olavi heard Inkeri scoff.

'Do you know where Inkeri dragged me last week?' Bigga turned and addressed the men.

'Well?' asked Olavi, though he had no desire to get involved in the matter.

'We went to interview the Chair of the Society for the Promotion of Sámi Culture.'

'I'm writing an article about the Sámi college.'

'You dragged me there for show!' Bigga snapped. 'I was an exhibit! I wasn't allowed to take a single picture. You only asked me what *I* wanted to study there and encouraged me to talk to that man. He thought I was trying to get accepted at the school!'

'Well, aren't you?' Inkeri asked.

'Grandpa!' Bigga cried, and stood next to Piera, who was following the situation across the brim of his coffee cup.

'You might at least give it some thought...' Inkeri implored her.

'Stop it!' Bigga shouted. 'Don't drag me into your stories. I'm not... an exercise in one of your books,' she hissed, and ran off. Inkeri put down her coffee cup in disappointment.

Piera took a sip from his own cup, then said: 'Didn't know you'd turned into such a staunch defender of the Sámi language.'

Inkeri glared at him. 'I'm just thinking of what's best for her.'

'Really?' Piera asked. 'Folk here are in two minds about that school.'

'Surely you defend it, too? It's such an important step for your language, your community. Besides, it's politically important; people are talking about it in papers up and down the country—and even in parliament!'

'Surprised they don't commemorate it in a postage stamp,' he mumbled.

'What have postage stamps got to do with this?' Inkeri sounded exasperated. Piera raised his saucer and turned to look at the canteen girl, who carried in a tray full of freshly baked cinnamon buns and placed it on the table. Piera muttered something and quickly walked away.

'That man is becoming senile,' Inkeri sighed. She turned to Olavi. 'Melander is planning to start a new magazine.'

Olavi raised an eyebrow.

'Really?'

'Yes, really. He wants me to work for him,' said Inkeri. Olavi looked her up and down.

'He said he'd like to publish a story about the Sámi college.'

'The one where you took Marja for show?' he asked. Inkeri glowered at him.

'The current paper didn't want to publish it, so we went all the way up there for nothing,' she complained. Somewhere, a plate fell to the ground and smashed, and everybody turned to look.

'How's your investigation coming along?' Olavi asked.

'It's not,' Inkeri mumbled, and she meant it. For the most part, Lotta Niinistö had gone silent, and now Koskela too. Her investigation into Saara had reached a dead end. Through Lotta Niinistö she had established that after the end of the war an arrest warrant had been issued for Väinö Remes, the interpreter whom Koskela had mentioned, but that was all she had found out. Everybody she tried to look for seemed to have disappeared like ash scattered in the wind. Having said that, after hearing Väinö Remes's name, Lotta had begun to show far greater interest in Inkeri's investigation. Now, instead of passing her information, Lotta had started regularly asking whether Inkeri had found out anything new about Remes and why she had asked for information about Olavi Heiskanen. Was Heiskanen somehow involved in all this? Inkeri looked at Olavi. He was staring in the direction of the broken plate, just like everybody else. His dark hair had been combed. He had got himself a pair of spectacles, and in general he seemed to have aged a little. She hadn't told Lotta anything about Olavi, and something inside her said this was the right decision.

For the first time, Inkeri had the distinct impression that Lotta Niinistö wasn't helping her out of the kindness of her heart and wasn't necessarily interested in Kaarlo's fate either. She recalled what Koskela had said. *Don't you find it at all suspicious?* Lotta had been an agent during the war, so there was no telling who she was working for these days. When all is said and done, was there anyone Inkeri could really trust?

'Melander's offer was very good. I could work as a European correspondent.'

'I don't know. Aren't you too old for that kind of thing?'

'I'm tougher than you think!' she laughed. 'What about you? The church is almost ready; all it's missing is the cross on the spire. What will you do then? Are you going to stay here? You should get yourself a wife, you know. Getting married makes people happy,' said Inkeri, then added wanly: 'Just look at me.'

Olavi burst into laughter.

'Do you know what our greatest passion was in Africa?' she asked.

'No.'

'Hunting animals. I took part in it too. Many times.'

'Is that how you got your ball of lion hair? Your trophy?'

'It is not a trophy. It's a souvenir,' Inkeri chuckled. 'In any case, it was a different time. Now, all these years later, it seems like nothing but vanity.'

Inkeri rolled her cigarette between her lips the same way Olavi sometimes did when he was nervous. Now she too had picked up the habit. 'There was a private garden near our house. It wasn't very big. But it was home to all sorts of creatures. Exotic birds, parrots, parakeets—crocodiles even.'

'And lions?'

Inkeri laughed. 'No, no lions. You can't imprison a lion. You either have to kill it or leave it alone. There were species from Europe and India too. And there was a young elephant. The calf had been found wandering around the nearby area, apparently lost, and was brought to the vet to keep it safe until they found a place for it in the zoo. The zoo had a magnificent garden. It had all kinds of plants and flowers—it even had its own gardener. You would have liked it,' she said. 'As you can imagine, maintaining a zoo is expensive—and laborious. From time to time, the zookeeper had trouble with the local tribes. Years after I had moved there, a rebellion broke out among the

Kikuyu workers. It was only a minor revolt, few people were hurt and, if memory serves me correctly, nobody was killed. Well, someone might have died, but none of us at least.' Inkeri spoke quickly, as if she was on edge. 'I was a different person back then.'

'We all were,' said Olavi quietly. Inkeri picked up the thought.

'Were we? What kind of person were you?'

'Different,' Olavi said plainly.

'You'll appreciate, there were lots of people who didn't accept the idea of keeping animals locked in cages. For some reason, somebody decided to attack the zoo. Everything went up in flames. The bars of the cages were prised open. The animals went into a panic. I happened to be visiting the owners when the fire broke out, and at first all I could hear was a loud noise and the earth trembling beneath my feet. Then I saw the monkeys and ostriches dashing from their prison. When we ran out to see what had happened, in the light of the moon we saw toucans and hummingbirds glimmering in metallic, copper hues, crowned pigeons and birds of paradise flying here and there without knowing where they were going. They flew into every last door and windowpane, until they came fluttering through their smashed glass roofs and soared to freedom, many fatally cutting themselves in the process. Wild predators attacked one another. Most of the animals died there and then, and the rest of them we shot. The rhinoceros's flesh provided food for weeks. Many of those species are extinct now.'

Olavi looked at her. Her hair now reached down to her shoulders; it was loose, only held in place with a single hairpin.

A few grey hairs had appeared, which Inkeri tried to lighten with citrus fruit she had got from a Swedish smuggler and, in the summer months, with dandelions. Nothing seemed to work. No one can stop time.

'My husband loved animals,' she said with a hint of sorrow. Olavi flinched. Though Kaarlo was always present, the mere mention of his name always took Olavi by surprise. 'He enjoyed the zoo, spent long hours there, but when the animals were released he was happy about it and didn't take part in shooting them. I did, though. In that respect, we were very different.' She gave a dry, melancholy laugh. 'After that he never hunted again, and in fact he began to advocate for bounty hunting to be completely outlawed.'

Olavi turned towards the stage, where he could hear the delicate strumming of someone playing the kantele.

'But did you know that the first time I ever saw a peacock wasn't in Africa?'

'But…?'

'In Helsinki.'

'Well, well,' Olavi laughed.

'It's true! It was in the Hietalahti harbour. I was only a small child then, my friend Lotta and I had run off to look at the sailors and dream of adventure. And there it was, strutting around and spreading out its majestic feathers, squawking at passers-by and frightening the donkeys until one of the sailors finally managed to capture it. Imagine, even I was a child once upon a time. Now I'm almost fifty, an old woman!'

'When I was a lad…' Olavi began theatrically.

'Do tell!'

Olavi thought about this for a moment. 'Very well. When I was a child, just a young lad, my father and I went out picking cloudberries on an open stretch of bogland. Father walked further out into the bog, and I stood on the spot looking around. I must have been about five or six. Then suddenly I couldn't see him, couldn't see him anywhere. I was afraid he might have gone off and left me, right there in the middle of the bog. The marsh was so open that there was nowhere he could have hidden without being seen.'

'What happened then?' Inkeri asked excitedly.

'I went off to look for him, of course. And I fell into the bog. All of a sudden, I dropped down and started sinking. Do you know what it feels like to fall into a bog? You instinctively try to scramble back to the surface, but the more you thrash around, the deeper you sink. And I was only five. Or six. And I was very short,' he said, his voice sombre. The sound of the kantele stopped, and someone clapped.

'At that moment, I was afraid. I've never been so afraid in my life. Ever. Not even during the war. I closed my eyes and prayed to God that if someone could pull me out of this bog, I'd do anything in return. Anything.'

'And…?' Inkeri asked, almost out of breath.

'Then, out of nowhere, my father appeared and hauled me up. I'll always remember that moment. My father was crying, and I'd never seen him cry, neither before nor since. Never. He claimed I was the one who had gone missing, and he and I never reached an agreement on the matter. It was such a peculiar thing. Most peculiar.'

'Is that why you started to believe in God?'

'I don't… What do you mean?' Olavi asked, and creased his brow.

'I'm sorry. I mean, you ended up reading theology.'

Olavi looked at her, puzzled.

'I'm sorry, I… I heard that you used to study theology.'

'Ah yes, that…' he mumbled, but didn't complete the thought, as Bigga-Marja appeared beside them eating a cinnamon bun.

'These are really good. Have you tried them?' she asked. Olavi seemed lost in thought as he took his lighter from his pocket, then lit a cigarette. Nobody answered.

'I've always wondered what it says on that lighter. Is it Russian?' asked Bigga.

'*Saara*. It reads "Saara" in Cyrillic letters,' Olavi replied without giving the matter any further thought.

'Saara?' Bigga-Marja cried. 'Did Saara leave it for us before she left? Why didn't you tell me it was her lighter?'

'I'm sorry, whose lighter is that?' Inkeri asked quickly. In a flash, the atmosphere had changed.

'The bloodletter's. The one who used to live in our house before Olavi moved in,' said Bigga, and she snatched the lighter from Olavi's hand and looked at it like a piece of long-lost treasure.

INARI

July 1944

T HE FRONT is not progressing. The border is moving backwards. The pain in my stomach is horrific. Even when I stand up, I crouch in agony.

July 1944

If my stomach doesn't start working properly tomorrow, I shall have to see the doctor. Nothing will stay inside. Kalle has smuggled me some herbal tea or something similar. Heiskanen has been taking care of my duties, though otherwise we are no longer on speaking terms.

There is a restlessness here among the men, and something has changed. They yearn to go home, they long for their wives, their women. Everywhere I go they talk about women, who has humped whom and on which leave, how many they have had and what it felt like. Some of the men here haven't even lost their virginity and they have begun to worry that they might never do so. One of them makes sketches of naked women, draws them lying beneath naked men, on top of them, to the side, in all imaginable configurations.

I have heard nothing of Saara for two weeks.

July 1944

A few partisan attacks at a camp to the north on the Finnish side of the border. Prisoners and guards all executed.

July 1944

I visited the doctor the day before yesterday, then once again today. The previous drugs didn't help alleviate my symptoms. The doctor scrutinized me from behind his spectacles. Only now did I see that his eyes were black, as though someone had punched him. But nobody has punched him.

The war had got to him.

There are, he tells me, seven different forms of faeces, the last of which is simply green gas. 'You're not quite there yet,' said the doctor, and ordered me back to work.

July 1944

Heiskanen hasn't spoken to me for a while, but now we have been forced to work shifts together, and we have been arguing about one thing or another. Our communication is nothing but quarrelling. Normally I would put up with it, but today it crossed a line. Heiskanen spoke about Saara, said that when he first arrived here he humped her as well, and that Saara always moves on to other men once she gets bored. 'She'll soon get bored of you too,' he said, his voice hard and dripping with scorn.

ENONTEKIÖ, 1950

'SAARA VALVA, the bloodletter, used to live in the house that I now own. Don't you find this simply extraordinary?' Inkeri paced back and forth in the restaurant and directed her words at Koskela, who was sitting at the bar counter. As she had been unable to get anything useful out of Piera or Bigga—not to mention Olavi—she had immediately contacted Koskela and arranged a meeting with him at the Pallas Hotel the following week. Conveniently, the inspector was planning to visit the hotel on business.

'And the name you gave me didn't lead anywhere either!' said Inkeri, exasperated.

'Really?'

'Really,' she snapped. 'A warrant was issued for Väinö Remes at the end of the war, but I don't know why, or where he ended up.'

Inkeri slumped down on a bar stool.

Bigga had told her that a bloodletter had spent a month living with them at Piera's house. This was the same woman who had been at the prison camp, the same one who might know something about Kaarlo's fate. According to Bigga, Saara was a very nice, exuberant woman. Meek and soft. Piera had just shrugged his shoulders. *Perfectly ordinary, she was,* he had muttered, and claimed he hardly remembered her.

Inkeri had taken out the photograph she had saved from the church foundations and shown it to Piera and Bigga. 'Is this the woman?'

The two looked at each other. 'Aye, that's her.'

'Do you recognize anyone else in this picture?'

'No, we don't,' said Piera. The fact that Saara had once lived at their house might account for why the photograph had ended up here, but it didn't explain why Olavi had tried to hide it. All Piera remembered was that Saara's residence card had expired by the end of the war, and this had caused her some concern. 'All she needed to do was go and ask for a new stamp or something. But she decided to leave—on the last day of the war. Upped and left, just like that. Folk didn't take kindly to foreigners.'

'Is that all?' Inkeri asked, jerking upright in frustration before slamming her hand on the table so hard that things hopped into the air. 'Are you absolutely sure you don't know any more about her?'

'It's not so strange that Saara lived here,' said Bigga-Marja in their defence.

'How so?'

'Well, all kinds of people have lived at Áddjá's house. During the war it was a guest house,' Bigga added quickly, and fiddled with her cradle-ball. Inkeri hadn't known that. She cast a sceptical look at Piera and Bigga.

But it was her conversation with Olavi that proved to be the strangest of all. Inkeri had wanted to talk to him in private. Olavi stuck to his story, claiming he had found the lighter. And not in the house, either, but further afield near the church construction site. He explained that he had been tasked with finding Saara after she was reported missing.

Inkeri asked whether this had anything to do with the fact that Saara might have been in the country illegally, and Olavi nodded anxiously. Inkeri had decided not to ask him about the photograph. Not yet. She concluded that, if it were the case that Olavi had in fact been asked to find this woman, that would explain why he had the photograph: he would have been given it to help his search. But why try to hide it later on?

What an impasse, what a mess. How was it possible that everybody suddenly knew who Saara was, but nobody seemed to know the first thing about her?

'I have accepted the fact that I might never find any information about my husband. And you know what? I've had enough. I've been offered a job at a new periodical. Perhaps I'll take it. At least it'll get me away from this backwater.'

Koskela observed her and closed his eyes. He caught the smell of smoke in the air. He opened his eyes again and looked out of the window. Spring was on its way; he could feel it during the day. Now, outside the darkness stretched into infinity. There was no blue moment, no stars, no Northern Lights. There was no light at all. Why was it always this dark? Why was it always so damned dark?

'You've been in Africa. Tell me, is the moon closer to the earth there than it is up here?' he asked. Through the window he saw the faint gleam of moonlight, but not the moon itself.

'No, it's not any closer.'

'Or further away?'

'No.'

'Neither closer nor further away,' Koskela nodded. 'Sometimes, it feels as though everything is so far away from here.'

Inkeri looked at him and pursed her lips.

'During the war, the camps often traded prisoners back and forth. It was commonplace.'

'Did they try to trade Kaarlo?'

Koskela smiled and nodded quietly to himself but didn't answer.

'That was the strange thing. This Remes wondered about it too at first, and tried to question it, kept asking why Kalle was at this camp and not the one in Parkkina…'

'Why would he have been in Parkkina?' Inkeri interrupted him.

Koskela looked right at her.

'What I'm trying to say is that, to my knowledge, he wasn't treated like the other prisoners,' Koskela explained. 'But as the war drew to an end, the Nazis started to become distrustful of us Finns. And for good reason. There was a substantial risk that the Finns, who had been at the camps, would tell their stories, and the Germans couldn't have that. Defence fortifications were constructed all across Lapland to protect against offensives from the Soviet Union and from the Finnish army. At the end of the war, orders were given to transfer Kaarlo to another camp. His treatment there might have been very different from what it was at Inari.'

Koskela leant back in his chair. Inkeri listened keenly.

'When Kaarlo was moved, I was the one assigned to hand over the prisoners. This was one of my typical duties, particularly whenever I was supposed to carry out a raid somewhere. On the way, I stopped at this very hotel—well, the one that was here before,' he smiled. 'Saara Valva accompanied me. That was a perfectly normal measure too.'

'But why?' Inkeri cried. 'And why did Saara Valva end up living at Piera's house—the same house where I live now? It surely can't be a coincidence.'

'There weren't all that many houses around these parts, even before the war,' Koskela noted. 'How is Piera, by the way?'

'Fine, I suppose. Age is getting the better of him. Do you know him?'

'Yes, I know him very well. We first became acquainted during the war. He was a great help. He has a granddaughter too—what was her name again?'

'Bigga-Marja. But nowadays she wants people to call her simply *Marja*.'

'Why?'

'Because it sounds more Finnish, apparently,' Inkeri grimaced. Koskela chuckled and started stuffing more tobacco into his pipe.

'I grew up in the forests in the north-east. Did you know there used to be lots of Sámi folk up our way too?'

'No, I didn't know that.'

'Well, nobody has been able to speak their language for centuries now. That language is long gone. But the old reindeer herd remains to this day.'

'What are you trying to say?' Inkeri sighed with disinterest.

'When I was young, nothing but a lad, I once saw a doe that had just given birth to a calf. There was something wrong with the calf. I don't know what, but it wasn't moving right. It just lay there, still covered in membrane, struggling with the kind of energy that only a newborn has. Sometimes I feel that's when we are at our strongest, our most courageous. It's as though life sucks the strength out of us with every passing year,' said Koskela, and placed his hand on the table. 'Well, a calf has to learn to stand and walk very quickly, otherwise the doe might abandon it. This calf couldn't stand upright. And the doe had given birth far away from the rest of the herd. In this unpredictable weather, getting separated from the herd could mean death. The doe had to make a choice: the calf or the herd.'

'Which did she choose?'

'The herd,' Koskela said gravely.

Inkeri stared at the grain of the wooden table.

'What happened to the calf?'

'It trotted after its mother a few hours later.'

Inkeri smiled. She thought of Alba, the white lion that had done everything to survive in this world. All of a sudden, she remembered the photograph still hidden in her pocket.

'Here. Do *you* recognize anyone in this photo?'

Koskela leant down towards the black-and-white image. When he spoke, his voice was colourless.

'Where did you get this?'

'That is Saara,' Inkeri pointed at the woman, and suddenly had another thought. 'And could this be Väinö Remes?' she asked, pointing her finger at the man in the Finnish military uniform. Why hadn't she thought of this possibility sooner?

Koskela looked at the photograph in silence, then repeated, his voice now sterner: 'Where did you get this?'

'My lodger left it by the church foundations. He was trying to hide it there.'

220

'Your lodger?'

'Yes. Olavi is his name. Olavi Heiskanen.'

Koskela slowly slumped against the back of the chair. His face was pale.

'May I take this with me?' he asked.

'No, you may not.'

'Why not?'

'Why do you want it?' Inkeri asked sceptically. She thought of Lotta Niinistö. She thought of herself and how there truly was nobody she could trust. Koskela was still looking at the photograph.

'No reason. You're right. You can keep it,' he said hurriedly. Inkeri looked at him. 'But I might have something of interest to you. I can bring it with me when I head out your way in the spring.'

'You're coming to Enontekiö?' Inkeri asked in surprise.

'Yes. I've just decided so.'

'Why?'

'There's something I have to look into.'

'And you have something for me?'

'Yes,' he said, deep in thought. 'Did you know that many of the soldiers at the camp kept a diary? Even though some of them could barely write properly, they still wrote every day. Quite simply so they didn't lose their minds, I imagine. To have someone to talk to, in a way...' he said, his words trailing off. Inkeri looked at him in bewilderment. Koskela picked up his cap and put it on. The darkness outside had deepened further. He still had to drive back to Rovaniemi this evening.

'When will you come?'

'Later in the spring. Perhaps a few weeks from now. Or in early summer,' he muttered. 'I'll tell you everything. I promise.'

INARI

July 1944

S AARA HAS COME BACK. I have been on leave all week-
end. My stomach pains subsided immediately. Saara said
it must have been down to my guilty conscience, but I think
it might have more to do with rotten food and bad hygiene. I
don't mention the things Heiskanen told me. I try to imagine
they never happened.

There are so many things that do not exist, though of course
they do.

July 1944

We have started talking about what will happen when the war
comes to an end. We played with the idea that I might take
Saara to the great wildernesses of Kainuu. I want to show her
the world. England. America.

All of a sudden, mid-conversation, Saara sighed against my
neck and said in a stony voice, 'You're not really going to take
me anywhere.' I asked her why not. 'I know what you men
are like. You'll promise the earth for a quick piece of skirt.'
I was suddenly unable to reply. I felt her stiffen in my arms,

then eventually she turned her back to me. Perhaps she was disappointed that I hadn't said anything. But I couldn't for the life of me think what to say. A short while later, I turned and took her in my arms again. Her hair smelt of soot and tobacco smoke.

July 1944

We have gone on an excursion up into the fells. Up here the alpine milkvetch grows like a weed. Only a few kilometres further north, nothing grows at all that rises above ground level. The highlands are covered with bilberries and lingonberries, pincushion plants, blue heather and trailing azaleas, and together they form a soft blanket of moss where you can lie down. It feels just the way I imagined.

Saara and I made love by a small tarn. How the water glistens in the leaves of the dwarf birches. 'The water is drawn to you,' Saara said quietly when she thought I had drifted off to sleep.

Even she dares not come closer to me than that.

July 1944

Now that the berry season is at its peak, we have planned to take a boat out to the islands in Lake Inari. The motorboat is broken and being repaired, so we've decided to build a new boat. The confounded crone Biret-Ánne helps us in this endeavour too. I don't understand how she seems able to do almost anything. Even Felde looked on in bewilderment at the decrepit woman in her red cap, her only company being her old herding dog, the one whose death she is eagerly awaiting. Felde appears to have given her permission to help us all the same. In recent weeks these motors have been more trouble than they are worth, because there have been problems with the cars too after the winter, and it seems that two motorbikes somehow sank through the ice and into the lake. Some of the cars simply will not start up, as though the winter had sucked them dry. According to Biret-Ánne, you can't trust machines. She is already busying herself, striding across the yard in her reindeer-hide boots, which she refuses to take off for any reason. Saara told me the boots were made from the scalp of Biret-Ánne's favourite reindeer.

July 1944

We are all hard at work building the new boat. I'm only too keen to help, anything to avoid meeting Kalle and Heiskanen. Now that I know everything, I too might be asked to help load bodies into a truck for night-time transportation.

Biret-Ánne is constructing the boat in the traditional way. Enough wood has been reserved for our project. The best wood for boats is from the female trees higher up on the plains, because trees that have grown elsewhere are too fragile, but this is the situation and we must make do with what we have. Mountain birch is still hardy wood and will give us a good keel piece.

July 1944

Kalle has been at the labour camps near the border, and when he returned he brought more wood for the boat. We still have to strip everything from these pieces of wood. They are riddled with bullets, pieces of iron, shrapnel. We must go over them with a mine detector before sawing into them.

There is a dance tonight. The prisoners are putting on a play. We shall see what comes of it.

July 1944

There are reindeer everywhere. They are mad for the mushrooms! They seem almost inebriated, wandering around looking for mushrooms, they can't see or hear anything but are always bumping into people and soldiers. Still, they must have some kind of survival instinct, as they always walk into the wind so that wolves, bears and wolverines cannot take them off-guard. Be that as it may, they should be looking out for mines and the like, but the poor things don't know how.

July 1944

We spent all day building the boat. My clothes stink of tar. I have commandeered some of the prisoners to help us. Biret-Ánne says the reindeer have started behaving strangely. They lie sluggishly in the roads and don't even have the energy to hump one another, though they are in heat.

The alpha stag has a wound in his leg from a mine, and nobody would have known if it weren't for Biret-Ánne. It wasn't even limping. Biret-Ánne noticed it from the movement of the creature's ear.

ENONTEKIÖ, 1950

I NKERI STOOD in the attic, warmed by the April sunshine, closed her eyes and sniffed the air. Spring had come quickly. The light had increased so much that it hurt her eyes. The school had been in recess for the last few weeks, and Bigga-Marja had been staying with her uncle and grandfather. Inkeri had overheard Piera complaining to Olavi about the girl. Apparently, Bigga had become impossible, and they had spent most of the holiday arguing. Still, they had ventured out on to the frozen lake once, watched the swans, listened to the crunch of what ice remained. When, in the first class after the holidays, Inkeri had asked the pupils to paint a happy memory, Bigga had painted a deep-yellow sunrise in watercolours, and two figures, one wearing a blue Sámi costume, the other a red one, and two swans flying across the sky. When Inkeri had visited the construction site and told Piera about the painting he had initially frozen, then, according to Olavi, spent the rest of the day whistling cheery melodies, one of which Olavi recognized as a song he had heard on the wireless.

Inkeri opened her eyes. Specks of dust hung in the attic air. When she closed her eyes again, she saw Kaarlo's dark silhouette against the horizon and Mount Kenya rising up in the distance. A fractured sky, flickers of sunshine, birds flying in an M formation. She could not let go of that image. She had forgotten many others, but not this one.

She thought of Alba. On one occasion, the lion had wandered far away to give birth and spent many days in the den. She had already had several litters, but none of them had ever contained a white lion. A week later, Alba finally left the den and presented her litter to the alpha male of the pack, then brought them to their father for his acceptance. If the male suspected that the cubs weren't his own, he might kill the entire litter, and the female too. This time, there was certainly some cause for concern. Inkeri remembered watching as Alba had mated with a different male while she was in heat. But her mate accepted the cubs all the same. And one of the cubs was just like its mother. Pure white.

She opened her eyes again. She had to be careful of the nails sticking through the floorboards as she peered into Olavi's room. She sometimes went into his room to amuse herself, on the off-chance that she might find something relating to her husband. Something interesting, something new, something that might tell her more about Olavi than he wished to reveal.

But every time she went into the room, she knew there was nothing of interest in there. In the corridor, opposite the room, was a small window, and on the window ledge she saw a flowerpot, the same one she had seen in all different places around the house. Sometimes it was on the ledge in Olavi's room, sometimes at the other end of the attic room in the direct sunlight or deliberately placed in the shade. She picked up the small pot, examined the branches, sniffed the soil. The plant was already flowering. It was small and delicate. Its intense, violet petals quivered as she replaced it on the ledge. Light filtered in upon the flower. Like hope.

One relatively mild spring day, Kaarlo was found badly mauled. It seemed he had gone off to gather butterflies, as his lepidopterist paraphernalia was left scattered across the embankment, a net, a magnifying glass, a butterfly book that he was always reading keenly. Kaarlo was brought to Inkeri, though in practice they no longer lived together. He was on the verge of death. Inkeri kept watch by his side all night, changed his old bandages for fresh, cooler ones, listened to his moans, injected morphine into his muscles, held him by the hand and prayed, played his favourite music on the gramophone, read him a book.

And grieved.

When she asked the plantation workers what had happened, she learnt that an elderly lioness had been spotted nearby, her muzzle red with blood. Inkeri had tried in vain to ask more, but nobody wanted to speak about the matter. Nevertheless, she could be very persuasive, and after a while she learnt that Kaarlo's attacker was indeed a white lion. Both the Kikuyu and the Somalis were afraid of the creature; they thought she was a ghost. But Inkeri knew better. It was Alba.

She didn't know what caused her more distress: the fact that someone she cared about had been attacked to within an inch of his life, or the fact that it had been caused by another soul that she cared for dearly. At some point, amid her grief she realized that, of all her lovers, only Kaarlo had been exactly what he had promised from the start: a friend who comforted and supported her. Nobody in this world knew her as well as

Kaarlo. It was the grief that finally made her understand what was ultimately futile and what really mattered. Companionship. Friendship. The bond that existed between them.

'A penny for your thoughts,' said Olavi, and Inkeri jumped to her feet.

'You don't want to know,' she said flatly.

'What are you doing up here?'

'I don't know.'

Olavi looked at the flower in her hand, touched its tiny petals. Inkeri rubbed her eyes.

'How are your eyes?' he asked out of the blue. She was taken aback.

'What do you mean?'

'Exactly what I said. You've been wearing sunglasses more and more often. Bigga told me there's something the matter with your eyes.'

Inkeri looked down at her hands.

'Indeed,' she mumbled, plucked a dead petal from the flower and thought about the lion's furball in her pocket.

Kaarlo had slowly recovered throughout that summer. They began talking about things the way they used to. Literature, stamp-collecting, photography. Art. Inkeri started painting again, taking photographs. Kaarlo commented on her work, guided her, shared his opinions. He had to rehabilitate his legs little by little before he could walk properly again. Before he could trust himself. Eventually, he learnt to walk quite perfectly, but he had become somewhat melancholy and dispirited. His exuberance was gone, and on more than one occasion Inkeri had found him staring into the distance, a pained expression on his face.

One autumn morning, Inkeri set off to find Alba. She had told the others that the lion was now a danger to the whole plantation, but everybody could see that she was harbouring a rage that needed to be quenched. Even Kaarlo didn't try to talk her out of it, though the creature was only following her nature.

Alba had grown old, she seemed perhaps scrawnier, more hunched, but she hadn't changed. She was with a different pack now, a pack that consisted only of females, probably her own children, sisters and cousins. Alba was the alpha female. Inkeri set up camp nearby, and from her vantage point she followed the pack for a few days with a pair of binoculars.

Inkeri knew that lions had one best friend. Their mate. The mate to whom the lion always returned after a long hunting excursion. The mate without whom they could not live and that they would protect and defend to the death.

How many times had Inkeri seen Alba returning to the pack, to one of her own kind? She had watched Alba nudging the other animal with her head, marking her scent and taking on the scent of the other, surrendering herself, playing and running so that the ground trembled; heard her purring so loudly that the sound carried all the way to the hideout.

Alba's best friend was another female four years her junior. And Inkeri knew that other female better than anyone else.

It was Alba's own cub.

'Do you believe in God?' she asked Olavi suddenly. He looked at her through narrowed eyes but didn't say anything.

'I do,' she continued. 'I believe in God because I have always got what I deserved. I was terrible to Kaarlo. I went out of my way to find the right word or deed to mock him, to sneer at him, his mistakes, his being. Everything. What kind of person behaves like that? A bad person. The truth was, I was envious of him. Of how free he was, how special and unique.' They looked on as the birds flew back and forth across the window, towards one another, then away again. The light seeping through the window had moved slightly to the right.

'Photography is the only thing that has ever been important to me. Light,' she laughed sorrowfully. 'Do you know? I never had any particular desire to go to Africa. I was afraid of the natives for years until I got used to them. Their languages were so peculiar—Swahili, the Bantu languages of the Kikuyu people, and what have you. Kaarlo spoke them all, of course.' Inkeri looked down at her hands and recalled the school in Kenya where she had taught the children English. Over the years, some of the children learnt the language so well that one could barely hear that it wasn't their mother tongue. *This is how we will get on in the world,* msabu.

'Before leaving Kenya, I visited the best doctors in the country. One of them told me this is a hereditary disease, that there is something wrong with my retina. He said it was like putting a scrap of cloth in front of a camera lens. If the worst comes to the worst, there might come a time when I am unable to see at all,' Inkeri whispered. 'The light. It hurts me. Imagine, the thing I love most in the world can cause me such harm.' Inkeri's voice was now nothing but a faint rasp of air. 'I believe I got what I deserved.'

She stroked the furball in her pocket. After all these years, it had remained smooth. Everybody thought the furball must have come from a far grander deed, that it was a trophy, that she had shot and killed a great, mythical animal. Speared its flank, put its head on display, its hide on the floor as a rug. How wrong they were.

One morning, Inkeri had encountered Alba's cub when she was out fetching water. Inkeri was standing on the other side of the river. Mist was rising up from the fields. The river grass was swaying in the breeze. The birds. They too were still asleep, their heads hidden among their feathers for protection. The white cat had been watching Inkeri for some time. She trusted her. But Inkeri felt no pity. She hit her with the first shot.

The war started the very next day.

And she hadn't seen Kaarlo since.

She began fervently pruning dead branches from the flowerpot. 'It's blossoming.'

'So it is,' said Olavi, a little surprised, though he saw the flower every day. 'Listen. Bigga told me you have a photograph. A photograph that belongs to me.'

Inkeri peered at him, raised her eyebrows as though she had no idea what he was talking about.

'What do you mean?'

'I… When I told you I was sent here to look for Saara… That's not the whole truth. I wanted to find her.'

'Do you know what happened to her?'

'In a way, I was hoping you might have found that out.'

Inkeri stared ahead, bit her lip.

'Saara…' Olavi began clumsily. 'She left something for me. Something important.'

'What was it?' Inkeri asked, and looked at him curiously. 'Is that why you're looking for her?'

Olavi lowered his eyes and whispered. 'She left something here, a piece of evidence that I could use if I was ever arrested.'

'And why would you be arrested?' she asked.

'Listen to me. That photograph. I must have it back. If it were ever to fall into the wrong hands…' Now Olavi's voice was grave. She could see that he wouldn't give in until the photograph was once again in his possession, that he would turn the house upside down to find it.

'But…' she began. 'What if I said I don't have it any more?'

'What? What do you mean, you don't have it any more?'

'That, perhaps, I gave it away.'

'You gave it…? To whom?' said Olavi, his cheeks pale, and Inkeri could see he was gripped by a profound terror. She bit her lip.

'What if I said I'd given it to Koskela? I gave the photograph to Inspector Tapani Koskela,' she said and looked up.

INARI

July 1944

'WHERE DO YOU come from, seeing as you speak so many languages?' I finally asked Saara. She leant her head back against the pillow.

Eventually even she decided to trust me. 'Akkala, that's where,' she replied, and laughed wistfully.

I looked up at the ceiling and tried to recall the map, all those tiny villages across the border.

'I'm Akkala Sámi born and bred, from between Alakurtti and Salla. We moved around a lot. I was only very young when we were forced to move to a *sovkhoz* in the village of Juonni. There were lots of Finns there too. When my parents died, I went to live with our neighbour Maija. That's where I learnt such good Finnish. And we spoke Russian, too, of course. I've spoken Inari Sámi and Skolt Sámi since I was little.'

I watched her. She looked somehow liberated.

'In the summer months, we lived near Lake Imandra, then moved down to the settlement in Akkala for the winter. I kept my traditional costume in the *sovkhoz*, though we weren't supposed to wear it.'

'What was it like?' I asked quietly, and gently brushed a few stray dark hairs away from her lips. Saara said nothing.

'I can't remember any more,' she said eventually, somewhat sullen, and I could feel her voice crack against the darkness. 'But my mother had a hat made of stiff red baize cloth. When she died, I hid it in a tin box and buried it. So they could never take it away from me.'

'How did you end up here?' I asked.

'When the war started, I pretended to be a Petsamo Finn, so I was evacuated to the Finnish side. Biret-Ánne took me under her wing when I arrived in Inari. It was risky. I didn't know where they would take us. One of the other trucks headed in the opposite direction, to Luujärvi in the Kola Peninsula. Later on, I heard that the people in that truck were taken straight to a prison camp. We'll just have to wait and see where they take us from here,' she said, hushed.

'I've never heard anyone speak Akkala Sámi. What does it sound like?'

Saara peered at me.

'That tongue has been silent for a long time now,' she replied, her voice now heavier than before. 'One of your prisoners can speak a few words of it, did you know that?' she laughed.

'Which one?' I asked, surprised.

'That Kaarlo, of course. Kalle.'

'Kalle?' I asked, and propped myself on my elbow. Saara nodded and chuckled.

'Believe me, I was confused too. He's never visited those parts. But at the turn of the century he used to belong to a group manufacturing propaganda leaflets, or so he says. The ones who made flyers and handed them out to the tribes in the northern border communities,' she explained.

'Flyers?' I asked.

'Yes, back when Finland became independent. We were sent some of them too. I suppose the idea was to bring the people in those border communities back into the Finnish fold before they became too Russian, too Swedish or Norwegian. But then the opposite happened. The propaganda frightened many people, and in Norway the Kven children were forbidden from speaking Finnish at school.'

'The turn of the century, you say. Just how old are you?' I asked with a quick smirk. Saara laughed and hit me with a pillow.

'Older than you,' she said, and lowered her head. I gave a laugh, then thought of Kalle.

'Does it bother you?' she asked.

'What?' I said, and at first I thought she was talking about her age. She looked up at me. 'No, of course not. Why would it?' I spluttered in confusion, quickly took out a cigarette and rolled it back and forth between my lips. I didn't know what to say. 'I don't think like the Nazis, you know that,' I said quietly.

'Do I?' she asked in an icy voice. 'Then how did you end up here?'

I stammered. 'I… Well, I wouldn't worry if I were you. The Nazis give the title of honorary Aryan to select individuals who are not genuine Aryans by birth,' I said, as though reading from a book, and at that moment everything changed.

Saara looked at me, her eyes cold and piercing. She pulled away. The colour had drained from her cheeks.

'An honorary Aryan?' she almost spat out the words, pushed me from the bed and told me to get out.

238

'I didn't mean it like that...' I began, but Saara took out the knife that I know she keeps under her bedside table and threatened to slice me open, from my throat to my groin, if I didn't leave right away. What else could I do? Her rage was so profound.

ENONTEKIÖ, 1950

B EFORE DEATH comes a premonition, a foreboding, an
omen. A black crow, a white reindeer. Olavi didn't believe
in omens. He didn't believe in anything else either. And yet, one
late-spring morning, he saw something that almost stopped his
heart there and then. He thought he saw a ghost reflected in
the windowpane. A familiar feeling instantly began clenching
his stomach, a sensation that he recognized as pain, the blood
drained from his toes and fingertips, his heart pounded.

He peered at the reflection, but a moment later it had disappeared. Instead, all he could see was a murder of crows and
a pine grosbeak which immediately fluttered up into the air, as
though taking fright at Olavi's gaze. Without this, he wouldn't
have looked out of the window at the dead pine tree, which
hadn't grown new branches or sprouted fresh leaves and hadn't
produced any seedlings for years. There in its branches sat a
solitary bird.

Without thinking of anything in particular, Olavi took the
binoculars from their pouch hanging by the corner of the
window, the pair that Inkeri had bought for birdwatching. He
raised the binoculars to his eyes and looked to the south-west.
Sitting on the branch of the old tree was a Siberian jay. Olavi
had seen these birds before but never paid them much attention.

He watched the bird for a long time, until he noticed something in the panorama that he hadn't seen before. Above the tree, three stars had appeared in the firmament. The Pleiades.

The ancient peoples believed that a person's age is predetermined and can be calculated from the Pleiades by counting the number of stars one can see with the naked eye. Olavi had once tried to see it in the sky, but he was unable to tell the stars apart. Piera claimed to have seen so many stars that he would live to be a hundred years old. He had already survived all manner of things. He couldn't die just like that, not of something mundane, like other people. When a life had been as adventurous as his, death would have to come up with something impressive, something that would overwhelm everything else.

But still, the very morning Olavi saw the Pleiades and the Siberian jay, Piera stopped breathing. When Olavi heard the news later that day, he immediately cast his mind back to what he had seen that morning. Some people believed that, after death, a reindeer herder's soul passed into the jay and lived on.

Despite Piera's indefatigable energy, death had come bluntly, trivially, the way death often does. His skin already appeared slightly shrivelled when they found him on his berth. He didn't look like he was sleeping peacefully or as if he had been in any pain. He looked simply lifeless. Deceased.

Olavi had been called immediately to help move the body to the church. It fell to Inkeri to break the news to Bigga-Marja and take her back either to the house or to her uncle. As he arrived at the main house, Olavi could smell death in the air. Piera had been brought inside, but his body hadn't yet been washed. That task was left to the churchwardens. Faeces had hardened on his trousers. His eyes stared up at the ceiling without seeing anything. One of them seemed to be pointing at an angle, down towards the lake. Olavi closed the eyelids; it felt uncomfortable looking a soulless man in the eye like that.

Piera's body was tethered to a horse-drawn sleigh. Before leaving, Olavi walked down to the lake and smoked a cigarette. The water glistened. Reindeer legs had been tied up along the wall to dry. The inner surface of the dangling shanks had been lined with strips of birch bark to stop the hide from shrinking; Olavi assumed that the herder's wife planned to turn the dried leather into a pair of shoes. This was a strange time to do it; people usually made their reindeer-hide shoes in late autumn. Maybe there was a need for them right now, or perhaps too many animals had been brought in for slaughter. Who knows?

Piera hadn't died inside the house, but in a tent-like shack erected by the lakeside hut. That's where he had been living. Olavi peered inside the hut. It smelt of juniper smoke, and here too reindeer meat had been hung up on a birch branch to dry. In the kitchen at the far end of the hut was a coffee pot and a cup. More dried meat. Olavi caught the same odour that he had smelt on Piera earlier. He never thought it could have become ingrained in him too so quickly.

Olavi stepped out of the hut, stood up straight and stared into the distance. The morning, brightening across the horizon, had stained the sky a sulphurous yellow. It was a beautiful day, too beautiful a day to die.

During the war, Olavi had seen more death than he had life. He remembered how years ago, on a morning very much like this one, he had come across a prisoner, who was half dead anyway, being tortured for fun. One of the guards had dashed to the poor soul's aid and appealed for the man's life. Commander Felde was drunk, either still from the night before or he was just getting started again. Perhaps he was high on medication. Saara once told him that many people in Germany used to take cocaine for recreation long before the war. After the outbreak of the war, the use of cocaine and amphetamines had escalated even further, and nowhere was this more evident than at the camps. Olavi remembered how Felde often drunkenly offered stimulants to the prisoners. This provided entertainment of its own, as many of the weaker prisoners succumbed to the effects of overdosing on the drugs, while the guards placed bets on which of them would survive and which would not.

But the guard who ran to help the agonized man was singled out for Felde's attention. The commander ordered the guard who had disobeyed him and another guard to tie the prisoner to the barbed-wire fence. Naked. Before long, the man was covered in insects, midges, flies and mosquitoes. Olavi recalled seeing something that looked like reindeer botflies on the man, though he didn't think they laid their larvae in humans. The insects ate away at his eyes, blood trickled every time he tried to swat the pests away, as with every movement the barbed wire cut deeper into his flesh. The other prisoners and the guards, and even some of the higher command, were all forced to watch the spectacle until they were given permission to disperse.

The prisoner survived overnight. The following morning, he was taken down from the fence. He stank of shit and piss, and the mosquito larvae had already begun to hatch. His skin was covered in blisters, raw, eaten, flayed. His mouth, gleaming wet and red, was the only distinguishable feature in his deformed face. The prisoner was forced to walk the five kilometres to the worksite. Walking was cumbersome and arduous, and after only twenty metres the man slumped to the ground and never got up again. One of the guards kicked the body. No movement. They felt for a pulse. Dead.

Olavi smoked a cigarette, looked up at the sun and contemplated life. And death. Before the war, he had never appreciated how many different ways there were to die. Before the war, death was somehow simpler, easier, an everyday matter. Anyone could die, at any time. There was life, and then there was death. But at the camps… There it was hard to tell the two apart. It was as though life were snuffed out only once the final glimmer of hope had gone. A long and varied path ran between life and death, a path laced with pain and fear. Hope was the last thing a person would latch on to. It was like hypothermia, Olavi thought. Just before freezing to death, you feel a soft, profound warmth.

He thought of Saara, how she had delivered the pregnant women's babies into a pail, thrown the sinews, placentas and slippery umbilical cords into the midden and burnt everything so that the smell wouldn't attract wolves, bears or other predators. *Or Nazis*, she once whispered, her hair hidden beneath a headscarf, her eyes a bright hue of violet. They were so large.

And then there was the operation in which, one way or another, they had all been caught up. He thought of the way Saara used to sew up bodies in the dark hours of the night, write down their age, race, sex, religion and any genetic defects in her notebook. Sometimes she helped pack them up and lift them on to the truck, though this was usually a job for someone else—Kaarlo, Olavi himself or the other Finn, the one that Olavi tried with all his might not to think about. The shipment sometimes included all kinds of organs, hearts, livers, eyes, all preserved in glass jars. He didn't want to think about everything that had been done to them since.

Suddenly, Olavi heard a grunt. He looked around. 'Matilda?' he whispered in disbelief. He walked round the lakeside hut, and behind it he saw the muddy pig lying on the ground, clumsily trying to clamber on to all fours. He waited patiently for the pig to stand upright, because the earth was very soft, wet and muddy. A moment later, the pig trotted towards him and sat down at his feet. When Olavi didn't immediately react, the pig began emitting small, high-pitched sounds and shaking her snout in all directions.

'What are we going to do with you…?' he muttered, crouched down towards the pig and scratched her back. Clumps of hair came away in his hand. He stood up and walked off, and when he reached the fence he turned to see whether the pig was following him. She was. On her way, she stopped to sniff the hut, then, satisfied that it was empty, continued after him.

Piera's son Lasse was waiting for Olavi with a horse, which he had borrowed from the church. Olavi untied the horse's leash from around the old dead birch.

'That tree,' said Lasse, and pointed to the old birch, which had long since shed all its bark. 'It's been standing there dead for three hundred years.'

Olavi turned to examine the hardened, grey tree.

'The scientists that have been running around up here have looked into it and they said the tree was born in 1333. Judging by the number of rings, it must have died quite young, in 1666. But it's still standing there, even though it's dead. It's the grandest tree in the whole area,' said Lasse, his eyes staring north-eastwards, where the tree line was only a few kilometres away. Beyond that nothing grew. No trees. Nothing at all.

Olavi stroked the trunk. Across the lake the sky was red. One evening, he and Saara had watched the red sun quietly smouldering as it sank behind the horizon. Saara had thrown a few more branches on the fire, perhaps to ward off the midges or the smell of death that hung around her. Drunken Germans shouted at her, asking her in Finnish what it felt like to shove her hand into a woman's quim. Saara spat on the ground and shouted: 'Just the same as pulling Herr Hitler's guts out through his arse. It's warm and slippery, and the heart comes out first because it's right by his backside!' The soldiers held their arms in the air as a sign they didn't want to have an argument and continued on their way.

A while later, he had taken Saara behind the barracks, opened her legs, caressed the moistness of her groin and easily slipped inside her. He came quickly, without making a sound. Saara wiped the inside of her thighs on her skirt, looked him in the eyes and ground herself against him one last time. Eventually, she placed his hands between them, tightly between her thighs and her vulva, and shuddered powerfully. After this, she kissed him on the lips, let go of him and nodded as if to leave, but he pulled her to him once more, held her in his arms, stroked her hair. He could feel her breath, her open lips against his neck. After this, they didn't say another word. There was nothing to say.

Olavi ran his hand along the tree trunk for a moment longer, its surface now soft and smoothed by the rain, then began checking that the coffin was securely positioned and fastened to the cart. He had gently nailed the coffin lid shut, leaving just enough space for air to pass through. He didn't want Piera to spend his final journey locked away.

'What'll happen to the pig?' asked Lasse, and looked at Matilda, who was watching both of them with her tiny eyes.

'She's coming along,' Olavi replied, and lifted the pig into the cart beside the coffin. He looked back at Lasse.

After this, he geed the horse into motion, waved and didn't once look over his shoulder. After a while, he felt something wet land on his upper lip. He wiped it away. It tasted warm.

Saara had once told him how, back where she came from, it was sometimes so cold in the winter that your breath froze into ice crystals. And it happened to speech too. Eventually, words frozen in the air slowly floated downwards, clinking brightly as they hit the ground. The villagers used to call it the whispering of the stars.

INARI

July 1944

I HAVE BEEN SKITTISH of late, unable to sleep. My hands are trembling. I cannot concentrate. I am at once worried about everything and about nothing at all. Heiskanen is constantly asking what's wrong with me. Sometimes when I have an attack, I can't draw breath. Though nothing happens, it feels as though I am constantly battling against time, that my body is waiting for something that I don't yet know is coming.

'What's the matter with you?' Heiskanen asks, then steps closer and holds out a mug of coffee. There's something so safe about the smell. I sit on the windowsill and gaze outside. On the side of the mug is a blue painted swallow and a flower that I don't recognize, though it looks terribly familiar.

A pennywort, perhaps.

A harebell?

I have lost my memory too.

July 1944

I dream that we get engaged. Saara and I. We give notice of the engagement in the local newspaper. We fill out dozens of forms and other paperwork, leave them at the magistrate's office, and I am even granted ten days' leave.

Saara's background has been thoroughly investigated. Her mother and father and grandmothers examined, their photographs scrutinized, their heads measured, and goodness know what else. Then I receive a letter from HQ, a letter that so many men have received before me. I have seen enough of them myself. Saara's race certificate. It reads: Sámi. The obstacle to our marriage is described as follows: fraternizing with degenerate elements is strictly forbidden and punishable in law.

The letter also contains a paragraph about race betrayal.

When I wake up, it feels as though I am suffocating.

July 1944

Everything is in disarray. A couple of Finnish journalists have been sent up here, a German and an American too, all reporting for an Australian newspaper. The commander ordered us to let a few prisoners free. The prisoners were instructed to pretend they were escaping, then some of the guards were to try and recapture them. It took two hours to film the whole charade. The photographers each wanted to film it from a different perspective, in a different place, a different light.

ENONTEKIÖ, 1950

D RESSED IN A BLUE SUIT, Tapani Koskela inspected the church carefully and smoked a cigarette. It was about six years since he had last walked along these streets. A lot had changed since then. The church was different too. The old, wooden church used to be situated nearer the shore. This new one stood proudly on the top of a hill, with views out across the lake and up into the fells. About a kilometre away, opposite the school dormitories, was the house that was his destination. To him, the church looked almost ready. It was grey and massive, though apparently it was still missing the cross, the altarpiece and the organ. The border-guard troops had started fundraising to provide a font. The organ had been donated from West Germany, of all places. Phlegm suddenly caught in his throat, causing a coughing fit. He had to clear his throat for a long time before finally spitting the phlegm out on the ground.

Koskela had parked his car outside the temporary police station. Though, of course, there were no police here at all. Naturally, he had heard about cross-border police operations to stop smuggling, but where were the results? Precisely. There was nothing to show for it. Nothing. Lapland was wild, a law unto itself. The rush of people prospecting for gold had caused quite a mess, but it wasn't the first such mess and it certainly wouldn't be the last. Petsamo was once Finland's very own Klondike. The people here didn't need law enforcement. They didn't need anybody. These fells had their own laws. The only things that governed travellers around here were cold and hunger. Koskela sighed and looked at the ground, where his spittle had disappeared into the earth. *Cold and hunger.* You could say, if that were indeed the case, then all was well with the world.

Perhaps.

He tugged his trousers up an inch or so. He had lost weight in captivity and hadn't been able to put it back on. Inevitably, he found himself thinking of old men slowly dying, first withering away and only then kicking the bucket. They had no appetite at all, no appetite for life. Koskela understood these old folk more and more. Even the smallest, most banal chores felt so exhausting that carrying them out required considerable exertion. And for what? You had to wonder.

In addition to his appetite, Koskela had lost the ability to sleep. He spent most of the night tossing and turning in bed, and around four o'clock he eventually gave up trying. Sometimes it was before four, sometimes later, but he guessed on average it was around four o'clock. Then he got up and walked to the dining table in his police residence, looked out of the small, dirty window and waited, waited for morning to come, for something to happen. Waited for life to move, in any direction. Every damn morning. It never moved anywhere.

But now it was moving. Now it had found a sense of direction, though he wasn't entirely sure where it would lead him. But it would lead somewhere. He wanted to believe that now he had the chance to bring to an end something that had begun a long time ago. *Olavi Heiskanen*; he recalled Inkeri's words and scratched behind his ear.

Initially, the messages Inkeri had sent him—first in prison and then at his home address—hadn't aroused his interest at all. He received letters from women almost every day, desperate women who wrote to male prisoners to garner attention, support or whatever it was they were looking for. Many women found a husband that way too. How curious it was. Then there were the village idiots and people who hated the police. It wasn't out of the ordinary to receive letters regarding old cases that had been closed long ago, or crimes that remained unresolved. It was only once Inkeri had called him and Koskela hung up on her that he had dug out her letter, read it and started to contemplate the possibility that this woman might be telling the truth after all. And if she was speaking the truth, what did that mean? Soon afterwards, Koskela managed to establish who Inkeri Lindqvist really was, and very soon he began to realize what this was all about—and he didn't know what to do about it.

Should he tell the whole truth, though that might land him in even more trouble? Should he keep quiet and deny everything, which might lead Inkeri to ask other people these questions, the kind of people he did not want digging around in the past? He was at a loss. He decided to trust his instincts and see what the future might bring. That was what he had done throughout his life. He had settled for his lot, he'd done what had to be done, and tried to act in the best way possible. He thought himself a just man in an often brutal world.

Sometimes he wondered if it might be best to take matters into his own hands and leave with his honour intact. Nobody would miss him. His wife had succumbed to cancer over a decade ago. During the war, he had lost Nessa too. *Nessa*, his reddish-brown Spitz, which was the best thing that ever happened to him. He would have understood if the dog had died of old age, or if someone had shot her, even by accident. But no. Cancer had taken the dog too. It was just a single, small tumour found at the base of the neck, but it was the devil incarnate. Cancer. Why couldn't it leave good, loyal animals in peace? Humans might deserve a thing like that, but not a dog like Nessa. Nessa was the kind of animal that, if Koskela had been the first of them to die, would have sat faithfully on his grave and died there when the time came.

Loyalty.

Indeed. Loyalty is the final measure of one person's relationship to another. Not how much they like or hate each other. Not whether they are the same flesh and blood or carved from the same tree. No. People are measured by whether one of them is prepared to make good on everything they have promised, to stand by someone in the face of death, to support them at their darkest hour. To kill, if necessary. There are very few people like this in the world. Koskela felt he could count them on one hand.

He looked to the north, then turned to face south, slipped his watch into his pocket. He still thought about Nessa every day. She had been with him at the camp in Alakurtti, where he used to work with Väinö Remes. On one occasion, Nessa had gone missing. She had run off following another animal's tracks and ended up on the wrong side of the border. Of course, nobody else at the camp seemed to care much. People were dying like flies. What use was it trying to rescue a dog?

But this Remes. The boy had lost his own father, and Koskela had become something of a father figure to him. Koskela had no children of his own, so he couldn't say whether he had become attached to Remes like a father to his son, but he wanted to look out for the boy all the same. At first, Remes was very sensitive. Such prissy behaviour usually irked Koskela, but over time the pale-faced boy became his closest friend. He had seen Remes writing in a notebook in his spare time, solemnly watching the sun rise and set, pondering life and death. Koskela didn't know what there was to ponder.

Perhaps the war was too much for people like that.

But there was certainly some truth in the notion that, though the war divided people, it also brought them together. After sharing such experiences, it was hardly possible to become closer to another person—both in sickness and in health.

Väinö had understood how painful Nessa's disappearance was. And so he set off to look for her—a solitary little creature, as the war raged around them—over uncharted plains, through wild, dangerous woodlands. And a week later he came back. With Nessa. Said he had found her curled up inside the carcass of a dead animal for protection. That's how clever Nessa was.

A few months later, they found the tumour on Nessa's neck, and in the end there were no other options but to put her down. She was suffering terribly. Remes had offered to help him with this too, said he would shoot her on Koskela's behalf.

But Koskela was the kind of man who couldn't live with a thing like that. He would regret it for the rest of his life. He needed to do it himself.

Nessa let out a small whimper as she died. He would never forget that whimper. He often thought about that sound as he stared out of the window at four o'clock in the morning.

He and Remes then buried the dog in the shade of a small tree. Now she was safe. Remes even carved her a wooden cross.

For all of this, Koskela felt a profound sense of gratitude towards Remes. But then Einsatzkommando Finnland was disbanded, and he didn't see Remes again for a long time, didn't know where he had gone. Koskela had been transferred back to Rovaniemi, but then one winter's morning—or was it spring, who can tell one season from the next any longer?—he ran into Remes in Inari. He was so pale that at first Koskela thought he had seen a ghost. And, in a way, he had. This wasn't the same boy he had taken with him from the Patriotic People's Movement in the wilds of Kainuu. Something about the boy had changed. His eyes were so black, his cheeks so gaunt. And he had become quiet too. Before, at least he used to say hello and good morning.

And then there was Saara.

Saara.

Koskela turned at the crossroads. The house looked just the same as when he had last visited. That was also the last time he had seen Väinö Remes. Back then, there was smoke and ash everywhere. Incinerated birds thumped to the ground in mid-flight, leaving black, smouldering soot smeared across the scorched earth.

Koskela shook his head at the memories and recalled the photograph that Inkeri had shown him. Photographs from that period simply must not exist. In the worst case, that photograph could lead people to him too. He didn't want to end up back in the penitentiary. If he played his cards right, he would be able to take the picture without arousing her suspicions. Unfortunately, Inkeri wasn't stupid. But he had a plan. First there was something he needed to ascertain. What Inkeri had told him… Was it really true?

Koskela had reached his destination. He opened the front door and knocked on the internal door in the porch. The hallway was heavy with the smell of chemicals. It seemed to be coming from the adjacent room, which he assumed must be the darkroom. A heavy sigh came from inside. Koskela opened the door and saw Inkeri raising her eyes from the living-room table. She was busying herself with a pile of papers. The room had changed over the intervening six years. Fashionable, patterned curtains now hung in the windows, music was playing on the gramophone, and a small box-like object, which Koskela recognized as some form of photographic equipment, stood on a tripod. He smiled, and his eyes fell on a large plant whose presence no longer surprised him in the least. In fact, it confirmed his suspicions. He closed the door behind him.

'You must be quite the botanist to keep a plant like that alive,' he joked, trying to maintain an air of levity. Inkeri looked first at the new arrival, then the fig sagging towards the floor, then at Koskela again.

'Yes. I must say, I don't understand much about it. But my lodger does.'

'Well, in that case your lodger is quite the botanist,' said Koskela, and took off his hat. 'What are you doing?'

'Making arrangements.'

'Arrangements? What for?'

'The funeral is tomorrow.'

'What funeral?'

'Áddjá's funeral,' came a voice from the hallway. Koskela turned and was taken aback at how much Bigga-Marja had changed.

'Bigga-Marja. Is that you?' he asked, his expression confused. 'I can hardly credit it. How you have… grown.' He had met Piera's granddaughter many times during the war, but the last and most powerful memory of the girl was from the day that he had been reminiscing about outside. Bigga-Marja had run up to them, her face dirty, stained with tears. The nearby camp was ablaze. Bigga-Marja told them there had been an explosion. *An explosion.*

'Well,' he began. 'I wonder if you remember me. I am—'

'I remember you,' Bigga interrupted him, walked straight to the sofa and curled up there.

Koskela suddenly didn't know what to do. Moments like that were rare. Perhaps it was this place, which reminded him so vividly of the war. Before the conflict in Lapland got fully under way, Koskela and a small group of officials had started visiting villages along the border. Partisan attacks had been happening all summer. *The summer of fear,* they called it. One incident in particular came to mind. It took place in the dying days of the war, or shortly afterwards, in September, once he had returned from Enontekiö. The group had come across a small village, by accident. Completely destroyed. Twenty-three bodies. The women had been shot and raped, both before and after death. Some had been tied to trees, left hanging there in grotesque positions, their wounds already full of maggots. The children had been stabbed in the back with a bayonet. The same thing continued right through the winter months. Though the order had been given to evacuate everybody, they didn't have time to visit every remote village. Those far away across the pathless moorlands were left to their own fate. The group came across several villages like this. Pillaged, burnt, destroyed.

Ash hovered above the bodies.

But even back then, he knew what had to be done. In wartime there were more laws, routines and rules than in peacetime. In peacetime there was freedom. *Freedom*. There were no rules for that. Freedom was chaotic. How could anyone live in a state like that?

'My condolences,' he said, so quietly that it was almost a whisper. Then he turned once more to Inkeri.

'Would you care for some coffee?' she asked him. Koskela looked around, imagining what would happen if Inkeri's lodger were to walk into the room right now. What would he do? he wondered. More to the point, what would *I* do?

'No, thank you. This is obviously a bad time. I'll come back later. I... I have something for you, Inkeri. But at a moment like this it would feel inappropriate. The things I have require explanation, and I hope, when the time comes, you will give them your full attention.'

Inkeri stood up. 'After the funeral, I have nothing but time.'

'I shall bring it after the funeral,' he said, and turned as if to leave, then stopped.

Inkeri looked at him, perplexed. Bigga-Marja was leafing through something that looked like a stamp collection.

'Your lodger isn't at home, then?' Koskela asked, keeping an eye on Bigga as he did so. Bigga-Marja glanced up, and for a moment the two caught each other's eye. Bigga bit her lip and looked down again.

'No. Why do you ask?' Inkeri wondered.

'It's nothing. I'm just interested in that tree and how he looks after it.'

'I can tell him you were asking,' said Inkeri.

'No, there's no need. In fact, it might be wise if you didn't mention anything at all,' Koskela hurried to add. 'And if it's not too much trouble, I'd very much like to attend the funeral. Your lodger… he'll be there too, I assume?'

Inkeri looked at Koskela, puzzled, her head tilted to the side. 'Yes.'

'Good.' Koskela nodded and left. He closed the door behind him and thought of Nessa's contented look whenever he scratched the spot on her neck where the collar had left a mark in her coat.

INARI

Aug. 1944

S AARA WILL NOT forgive me. She will not speak to me.
She won't even look at me.

Aug. 1944

The boat has been assembled, sealed with tar, oiled both inside
and out, and now it is ready. Biret-Ánne and I took it on its
maiden voyage to a nearby island. There is a cave on the island,
and inside the cave there is still permafrost, ice that has never
thawed and that has been there from the time when this lake
first appeared.

But when I stepped up to the mouth of the cave, the ice
began to melt straight away.

Aug. 1944

In the evening, the same photographers seemed to be having
a party. Apparently they are leaving tomorrow. They wanted
to take more pictures of us. Heiskanen, a few prisoners and

even Commander Felde were assembled for a portrait. Saara agreed too, and Biret-Ánne pushed her way into the picture with a satisfied smirk, barging right in front of the doctor.

I watched them from a distance, though I too was invited into the picture. Saara looked at me stony-faced, so full of hatred. Heiskanen lightly touched her on the shoulders, whispered something in her ear. Then Saara looked at the camera, and I was sure her expression would crack the lens.

Aug. 1944

I cannot get Saara and Heiskanen out of my mind. I cannot sleep, and I cannot do anything while I am awake either. There is something between those two, something that I can never have. What does Heiskanen have that I don't? I must do something. I must recapture my position, clear Heiskanen out of the way.

Aug. 1944

Kalle was taken away with the night-time transportation. I led him out, handed him over to Koskela at the county jail. At the commander's orders. Heiskanen knew nothing about it. He panicked and lost his temper at Felde.

I lie awake, clasping Biret-Ánne's cradle-ball in my hands and wishing I was somewhere else.

Aug. 1944

Today we were ordered to construct a train line to the fortification. Felde says he has enlisted Heiskanen to help too.

All of a sudden, words spilt from my mouth to the effect that Felde was right all along. The lies dried my lips, but I continued nonetheless. I told him Heiskanen should be eliminated. I lied and said that I knew he was passing information to the Finnish police.

Felde gave the order to kill him.

Aug. 1944

There was fog this morning. Mist. Heiskanen and I are getting the prisoners ready for departure. He doesn't speak to me. He knows something is afoot. He takes a step away, and I take two, alternately towards each other and away, like a dance, a mirror image. This time I am ahead of him.

Aug. 1944

It is warm, but there is a new chill in the air, the kind of weather that stirs up the stuffiness of the passing summer. The earth is pungent, it smells almost the same as in the springtime, but now there is something else in the air too. I am waiting for something; I don't know what.

I wait for death.

I wait for life.

Aug. 1944

We walked past Saara's house in the village. I delivered a letter to the letterbox. Inside the envelope, I sealed the gleaming silver cradle-ball and a small cutting from the alpine rhododendron.

ENONTEKIÖ, 1950

BIGGA-MARJA had difficulty hiding her sobs. The grave-yard was situated about five hundred metres north of the church, where it spread out in a vast sea of lichen. The crosses on the old headstones had been battered by the wind. Some of the names on the stones were ones that Olavi had never heard before. Further off came the sound of construction. Completion work on the village hall paid no heed to the clock.

Olavi heard neighing, turned and saw a scruffy bay horse. It was a good thing that the horses, which the state had comman-deered for the war effort, were still available to hire, otherwise there would have been a shortage of work horses. But it was expensive, and the price hadn't come down, not even during the most feverish years of reconstruction work.

The eulogy began. The priest's voice pealed across the grave-yard. The locals were dressed in their finest clothes. Though Olavi knew that it was customary to use more reserved Sámi costumes at funerals, he couldn't help admiring the array of colours around him. Embroidered scarves and tassels, sleds with bridles decorated in gold and silver, glinting as bright as the sun. Bigga-Marja was wearing her mother's old dress, which Lasse's wife had taken in so that it fitted properly. The deco-rative trimmings along the seams and braids across the chest and shoulders showed which clan she belonged to. Ribbons ran up her ankles, the tassels on her shoes quivered with every step. Olavi thought it strange to see the girl dressed up like this. As he looked at Bigga, he realized he hadn't seen the village so awash in colour for a while, for years. In fact, the last time was probably at the casting of the church's foundation stone. Things had changed a lot, people had changed. It felt as though an eternity had passed since then.

Olavi stood up straight and pulled down his jacket. He was dressed in a dark suit and a hat suitable for the occasion, which he took off then put back on his head. It was as though this was the hat's sole purpose: that one could take it off as a show of respect while the coffin was lowered into the earth. Inkeri too was wearing a hat fashioned mostly from dark net fabric and featuring a shiny, black-and-green feather. Their attire was like a remnant of a bygone age, a time before the war, before every-thing. In addition, Inkeri wore a dark-blue diamond necklace, which aroused more than a few raised eyebrows. Olavi hadn't imagined that Inkeri owned such jewellery. He realized he knew very little about her.

Inkeri's eyes glanced here and there across the assembled crowds as though she was looking for something. Olavi knew she always kept sunglasses in her handbag, and he could tell from her expression that her head ached though she was trying to conceal it. Her fingers were yellowed with tobacco.

'We therefore commit his body to the ground; earth to earth, dust to dust, ashes to ashes,' the priest intoned. The text on the iron cross read: *Beloved in Life, Mourned in Death.* There were lots of people in attendance. Piera was a well-known man. There was a sense of helplessness and resignation in the mourners' expressions. Fear too. Such was the nature of grief. A solemn acceptance.

An amen echoed across the trees, and Olavi pressed his hat on his head.

Inkeri walked towards him.

At first, Olavi didn't realize who it was standing next to Inkeri. He looked at the man, looked him right in the eye, and thinking about it afterwards he didn't understand how he could have seen so little, so poorly. Perhaps time had changed Koskela too much. No. No, it had not, he concluded. Despite having obviously lost a little weight, the inspector was the same as before. At the same moment, Olavi realized that he too had changed over time.

The two men shook hands. Inkeri watched their gestures attentively, but neither gave more than the most perfunctory of introductions. It was as though they had never met each other. That was just as it should be. During the war, none of them was supposed to be where they had been.

'Tapani Koskela.'

'Olavi Heiskanen.'

They looked at each other in silence as people walked past them. One of the guests approached them and tugged at Inkeri's sleeve, and she looked visibly irritated at having to leave the men alone. Bigga-Marja peered at them with interest, and Olavi knew only too well why: she alone knew that the two men had already met.

'Do you fish?' Koskela asked out of the blue. Olavi looked at him, puzzled.

'No, not to speak of.'

'Shame. I've got a boat I'm trying to sell.'

'A boat?'

'30,000 marks. It's a fine boat.'

Olavi put a cigarette between his lips and lit it. His hands were shaking. Bigga-Marja fiddled with the ribbons on her headscarf, and just then someone came up to her, said a few words in Sámi and asked who she was.

'*Mu namma lea Hágas-Bierá Biggá-Márjá,*' Bigga curtly introduced herself.

'*Leago Hágas-Bierá du áddjá?*' the questioner continued. Bigga nodded and turned, and the guest hurried away.

'What colour is it?' Olavi asked.

'Green. It's green. Made during the war, August 1944. The PoWs painted it,' Koskela explained, puffing on his cigarette. Olavi felt as though he was sinking into a silent mist. A bog.

'Propeller?'

'Added one later.'

'Doesn't the inspector know you shouldn't buy boats just for the joy of fishing these days? You could get yourself into trouble,' Bigga-Marja interrupted their conversation, her arms folded. They both looked at the girl in surprise. The corner of Olavi's mouth was twitching.

'I'll write you a permit to show to the police if anybody asks.'

'Best make sure nobody asks questions in the first place,' Olavi remarked.

'Suit yourself,' Koskela smiled. 'I'll give you a good price.'

Far across the horizon, large clouds had begun to gather above the fells. Rain. A thunderstorm. Here it was still sunny.

How strange that the weather could be so different yet so nearby.

'Well, I'm sure we'll be seeing each other. Soon enough,' Koskela said, then walked off towards the table of refreshments. Bigga and Olavi watched as he came to a halt beside Inkeri and the two began talking. Bigga looked at Olavi.

'What do you think they're talking about?' she wondered eagerly.

'The weather, I imagine,' Olavi quipped, and took out another cigarette, lit it.

Bigga held out her hand. Olavi gave her the box and the lighter. They listened to the murmur of the wind, looked at the moss-covered graveyard and the hay, its tips almost touching the sky. They could hear the guests beginning to take their leave. The cars, horses and reindeer kicked up puffs of dust from the path, and the sun slowly moved to the right. Clouds glided across the fells.

INARI

Aug. 1944

T HE FLOODWATERS RECEDE to reveal human corpses, white, half-eaten eyeballs with irises in all different colours. The guts the prisoners have defecated float on the surface of the sodden land like adders in the sand during the summer months. When you step on them, they squelch like worms.

The rain continues, causing further flooding. The earth is sludgy, you can't step anywhere without getting your feet wet, and all around us everything is black and empty. There is nothing else. Silence. I might have fallen down. I'm not entirely sure, but I am muddy and dirty. I have hit my head. Either that, or I have been shot.

As I stand up, I wonder: did the birds ever sing at all?

Blood trickles from my left nostril. The bleeding continues for over an hour. My face is red with blood. The birds have all disappeared. That night, I come down with a fever. My bones strive to force their way out of my body. Wasps sting my eyes, I can hear their buzzing and try to swat them away. I am shivering and haven't slept at all, though the latter cannot be true because someone has brought a bowl of water and left it beside my bed, the way they might for a dog, and placed a rag over my brow, and I don't remember any of this happening.

I'm not sure who it was. Perhaps it was nobody. Perhaps I am imagining everything. Perhaps I did it all myself. Or maybe it was Saara. But I know it wasn't her. She doesn't exist. She has gone. Maybe I imagined her too. Olavi isn't here either. Kaarlo is gone. There is nobody here. I am no more. Everyone has died. Everyone. I didn't kill anybody, I shout in my sleep.

I visited the doctor; I don't remember anything about it, but so I've been told. Who was it who told me? I don't know. But that's what I heard. The drugs I was given last time were no longer available. I was given sixty pills of something or other. I don't know what they are. I have just taken a handful of them. A soft, light wave washes over me. A rush. I leap into the abyss, and the emptiness lasts for so long that my stomach feels clenched and sore. I wake up to my own vomit. It has been two days since I last heard birdsong. I think it was a titmouse.

No, it was five days ago, and it was a hazelhen.

A full week has passed.

The mare has run away and taken all the birds, sitting on its back as though perched on a branch.

Nobody has spoken to me. Nobody says anything to me. The memory of myself fades, and I disappear. The mirror image is empty, like a deserted house. For the first time, I realize I have staggered out into the vegetable garden. I have spent several days out here. I eat handfuls of earth, not carrots or potatoes. They are all gone.

I vomit.

I empty my bowels.

Green gas, I think, but there is no longer a doctor here to witness it.

I sleep in the barn, I think.

I'm not certain, but I believe so.

I eat hay like a horse.

I don't know. I cannot trust myself.

I eat earth. The soil smells of iron between my fingers. Ferrous and sickly sweet. It smells of blood.

Is anybody there? I shout so loudly that the trees fall.

I have stepped across the remains of human bodies. A bear has mauled one of them, slashing it open. It didn't notice me, because I am dead too. There is something on the bottom of my shoe, something slippery and gleaming.

I will lie for ever where she kissed me for the first time. I am infinite.

Rain and wind.

Unending.

Day after day. It floods the barn.

The birds are all dead.

ENONTEKIÖ, 1950

O LAVI PRICKED UP his ears. He could hear distinct footsteps heading towards him. 'Hello there,' came a choked voice. The man sounded out of breath. Otherwise, the voice was firm.

'Hello,' said Olavi without turning to see who had arrived. 'Did you know this area is full of ancient potholes that the local herders used to catch reindeer?'

'I didn't know that,' the voice replied. The man stepped out, sat down next to Olavi, kicked the dust from his feet and took out his pipe. 'Quite a place you've chosen here.' Koskela inhaled deeply, coughed, then caught his breath. The early-morning silence was intoxicating.

'Bigga give you the message?'

'Bigga gave me the message.'

'Did you ever imagine it would end up like this?' Olavi asked once Koskela had steadied his breath. 'That of all the people in the world, the two of us are still standing.'

'No,' said Koskela. 'I can't say I did.'

'What's the probability of that, do you think?'

'I don't know. Not very high. Ten percent?'

'Ten…' Olavi looked at the hip flask in his hand. *Ten…*

'Or eight. Let's say eight.'

'Whatever it is, it's pretty damn slim.'

'Vanishing, frankly,' said Koskela. 'I thought you'd be in America by now.'

'You ended up in the penitentiary.'

'That's right. So the powers that be decided.'

Olavi gulped. 'I was afraid you would turn me in.'

'But I didn't.'

'No, you didn't.'

'It crossed my mind. Back then. But not now. I thought, what difference would it make? Nobody would have found you, because you were supposed to be in America. Something told me not to breathe a word, so I didn't.'

'Did anyone ask?'

'About what?'

Olavi smoked his cigarette. Swallowed again. 'You know what.'

'They touched upon it, in a roundabout way. But they had no specific information, nothing watertight. The former staff from the Paatsalo Unit took care of putting the case together. There are still a few agents looking for me, but they don't know anything concrete either. They don't have the resources.'

'Right. It's just, I thought you were on their side.'

'I was. Still am. But some things aren't worth bringing out into the open.'

'We didn't do the right thing.'

'No. *You* didn't do the right thing. But it's all about the bigger picture. They're hunting down the smaller fish, trying to catch as many as possible so they can make people believe they don't need to catch the big fish. That's their plan.'

Olavi picked up a stick and began scraping patterns into the dirt. The sun shone across the row of fells. The clouds had dispersed. The early-morning air carried the scent of flowers.

'Did you know Kaarlo's name is mentioned in the Red Cross's prisoner list?'

'Yes. I'm the one who wrote it down,' Koskela replied.

Olavi stretched his toes and opened his lunch box. 'I brought some food.' He pulled out a piece of bread, handed it to Koskela and pointed at the fire, where a small pan was bubbling. 'There's coffee over there.' He poured Koskela some coffee in a burr cup, then poured for himself too.

'You still see people crossing those old trails. They're mostly just ancient reindeer-herding trails, but some people cross them for the sheer fun of it. It's peculiar,' Olavi pondered. 'From here, it looks like nothing but rocks and boulders, but when you walk back down into the valley it's like a jungle. At this time of year, the waterlilies and globeflowers are in bloom, and all kind of flowers you don't encounter very often.'

'You and your plants,' Koskela joked. 'I have to say, I was damn happy to see you, if a bit surprised.' He gave a cheerful laugh and patted Olavi on the back.

'Yes. Me too,' said Olavi and smiled.

'Why the hell are you still here? Did you find out whether Bigga-Marja was telling the truth?'

Olavi lowered his head and tried not to remember. The smoke. The blackened, charred birds. 'She probably was telling the truth.'

'And you still decided to stay?'

274

'Yes,' said Olavi, hushed, his head hanging. 'Perhaps I thought, there's still a tiny chance. Maybe Bigga saw it all wrong, maybe she was lying after all. She was just a child back then; children make up all sorts. I suppose that's why I gave Inkeri Saara's name. I wanted to hold on to that thought.'

'And do you still think that?'

'I'm pretty sure Bigga was right.'

'How sure?'

'Not far off a hundred percent.'

Koskela smacked his lips.

'Does Inkeri know what happened to Kalle?' asked Olavi.

'None of us knows what happened to Kalle,' Koskela reminded him.

'Why did you help Inkeri?' Olavi's tone was now somewhat accusatory. Koskela guffawed with laughter.

'Why did *you* remain living under the same roof as her?'

'You know what they say about enemies,' said Olavi, and gave an involuntary chuckle.

'Best to keep them close.'

'Exactly.'

'But I don't think Inkeri is an enemy after all,' said Koskela.

'No, she's not,' Olavi admitted. He smelt the smoke and prodded the fire, as the midges were beginning to swarm in the air. The two men sat quietly for a long while, each lost in his own thoughts, each thinking almost the same.

'In the capital, they've started drawing up plans for some kind of Sámi register,' said Koskela, breaking the silence.

'What?'

'They've started planning a register of the Sámi people.'

'What's that?'

'It's supposed to document the people, to know who is a Sámi, how many there are, where they live.'

'I see.'

'The state wants control of the forests up here, the peat bogs and what have you, they want to use the natural resources for their own ends, but these indigenous folk are a bit of a legal spanner in the works. The state wants to know what rights they have, and how it can get around them,' said Koskela.

'Well, who is counted as a Sámi?'

'It hasn't been defined yet. Most probably anyone who speaks a Sámi language as their mother tongue.'

'Is that so?' said Olavi. 'At this rate, there won't be any left soon. Even Bigga hardly speaks it any more.'

'I told Inkeri too, said she should write about this for a change. Maybe the new magazine she's been talking about might run an article about it. She could at least forget the prison camps for a while.'

'Is it thanks to you that she's become so keen on the subject?' Olavi smirked, and thought back to the article about the Sámi college that Inkeri had put so much work into and that had caused such a rift with Bigga. 'I don't know. Maybe it would be a good thing for someone to write about the camps. It's a while back, now. Everyone's dead.'

'*You're* not dead,' said Koskela, now serious. Somewhere far in the distance came the high-pitched squawk of a bird. Koskela's expression was grave.

'Does it still bother you? You've nothing to regret.'

Olavi looked at the fire, blinked, unable to respond. 'I heard that the man who took delivery of the shipments was sent to the penitentiary. For mutilation of bodies or something like that.'

'It's true. You might meet him sooner than you think if you stick around here.'

'And who will make sure of that? You?'

'It's pure luck that it hasn't already happened,' said Koskela, staring up at the sky. He touched his pocket, thought for a moment, but didn't take anything out.

'The photograph that Inkeri has,' he began. 'The one taken right at the end of the war. The one that just happened to show everyone responsible for the operation. Saara, the doctor—'

'What? Inkeri told me she gave you that picture!' Olavi cried.

Koskela looked at him. Laughed. 'Did she now? No, on the contrary. She didn't want to give it to me.'

'Why did she lie about it?' asked Olavi, his brow furrowed.

Koskela looked down at the ground. 'Why indeed…' he muttered. 'Maybe she wanted to lure you, get you to show your hand. Anyway, the photograph. We were supposed to burn and destroy *all* documents. That photo is a very significant document,' he said under his breath. Olavi stopped drawing with the piece of wood. 'Why does it still exist? And how did Inkeri get hold of it?'

'Bigga-Marja…' Olavi sighed. 'You had already left by then, but Bigga-Marja told me that Saara had taken something back to the camp and said I should go and find it. At first, I didn't know what she was talking about. And, of course, I thought everything had been destroyed after the Germans left. But then I found it. The photograph had survived, framed, hidden inside a tin box. Initially, I didn't realize what it was or what it meant, but I knew that Saara had left it there for me. Until eventually I realized it was a free ticket.'

'A free ticket?'

'Yes. A free ticket for me. I could prove who was involved in the operation, maybe even use it as leverage if I were ever caught. It's like you said: if someone started investigating those people's backgrounds, they would find out that the Finnish soldier in question was supposedly discharged in 1942. And yet there he was, standing next to the Nazis, surrounded by prisoners. But I'm not in the photograph,' said Olavi. Koskela nodded and lowered his eyes.

'And I was thinking...' Olavi swallowed quietly. 'Well, I suppose I thought I would let the matter go. Three years had passed since the end of the war. At some point, I needed to let it go. But I couldn't make up my mind. I couldn't bring myself to destroy that photograph, but I couldn't bear living with it either. The thought of it bricked into the church foundations gave me a little comfort. The truth would be there for all to see, if only they knew where to look for it.'

'The doctor was the missing link,' said Koskela abruptly.

'What?'

'The doctor was the nexus for everything else. He was the one with contacts at the universities and further afield. Not Saara, though there were plenty of people who thought it was her. That was just gossip. The doctor was renowned for his ideology, he had conducted many dubious experiments and he was associated with the Committee for Racial Purity, but there was never any proof of anything beyond that. After the war, he fled to Sweden. He's still there.' Koskela cast down his eyes dejectedly. 'And the folk here don't know anything about you?'

'No. Nothing,' said Olavi.

'Except Piera?'

'Piera knew a thing or two. But even he didn't know my real identity.'

'What about Bigga-Marja?'

Olavi didn't respond but looked on as the wind scattered the patterns he had drawn in the ashes, as though they had never been there at all. 'What should we do now?' he asked.

'You know what has to be done. You don't have many options. Inkeri's questions have raised suspicions with the kind of people you don't want coming after you,' Koskela replied calmly through the wind. Olavi took out a cigarette, rolled it back and forth between his lips.

'Maybe you should think about buying that boat. It'll get you across the border. You can have it for free, if you want. After all, you made it, Väinö,' Koskela murmured.

Olavi lowered his head. The sun came out from behind a cloud. The shadows shifted position right in front of their eyes. The birds broke into their morning song. Somewhere, people were waking up, washing themselves, pulling on their clothes, crossing the yard and beginning their lives.

INARI

Sept. 1944

I WAKE TO A SWEET, cloying smell. It is unpleasant, fusty and filthy, it fills my nostrils, my mouth and ear. With the other ear I hear someone urinating into a metallic bowl, and this is the sound that finally wakes me up.

I have been brought to a hospital.

I call over a nurse and have my belongings brought to me. The nurse won't let me discharge myself. She explains that Inspector Tapani Koskela brought me here. *What day is it?* I ask and she tells me. It is September.

I am listless. I cannot remember anything of the last few weeks. I'm afraid she might hand me over to the authorities, that she will tell them what I have done, and they will execute me round the back of the police station. I will be no more.

ENONTEKIÖ, 1950

*T*HE RUSTED RUMBLING *of the railway, iron against iron. Dead
branches on the ground. A signpost decaying in the mud. He couldn't
make out the name, but he knew it already.*

Olavi snapped out of his thoughts, gazed out of the cabin
window at the sun and the horizon. Koskela had returned to
his temporary residence at the Kolehmainen guest house to
spend a few days awaiting Olavi's decision. Three at most.
Olavi knew what he had to do. But first, he had to get used to
the idea. He could hear Inkeri whistling; as usual, she didn't
even realize she was doing it. She was busying herself at the
typewriter, but she wasn't writing anything. Instead, she was
examining the photo album that Bigga had put together, the
portfolio that she had apparently been working on all year, or
at the very least from the time when she was able to use the
camera. She must have developed these photographs in the
school building; either that, or she had done it in secret here
at the house, as neither Olavi nor Inkeri had any inkling of
her project.

Bigga, meanwhile, was lying on the sofa, quiet and brooding,
as was her wont these days. In the reflection in the window, Olavi
could see that she was holding the lion's furball in her hands,
nervously fidgeting with it. He had seen the album first. Bigga

had come in and shown it to him, proudly but with an air of embarrassment. Olavi thought it was magnificent. Genuinely. It was a three-part work. At the beginning, she had glued dried flowers to the first page of each opening; Olavi recognized these as the flowers she had gathered years ago, flowers deemed unsuitable to adorn the garden. On the opposite page was a photograph of the same flower in its natural habitat. There were photographs of traditional villages and people in Sámi attire. Photographs of gorges, isthmuses, bends in the river, tall, rocky waterfalls and deep ravines; places where flowers blossomed and others where nothing grew at all.

Then gradually, almost imperceptibly, portraits of people began to appear. This was the third part of the album. Photographs of Olavi. Photographs of Inkeri. Images of Olavi building the new church, moments frozen in time, Olavi discussing whatever it was he was discussing with Piera, a cigarette dangling from the corner of his mouth. Laughter. Joy.

Inkeri. Inkeri taking photographs on the fells. Inkeri writing her articles. Inkeri pointing at the Sámi folk, showing them how to pose for a picture. The Quakers. People playing volleyball.

Bigga had photographed *them*, going about their business. Suddenly they were everywhere, all around. The strangest thing was that Olavi had never seen the girl with the camera. Not once. How could he have missed this? He scratched his head and turned to look through the window at the green landscape beyond. The water was still.

'When did you take these?' Inkeri asked, her cheeks pale. Olavi assumed that she must be thinking the same as him: how had they missed this?

'I wondered... I've been thinking about applying to a school somewhere...' Bigga replied. Olavi continued to watch her, reflected in the windowpane.

'A school? Which school?'

'I don't know. An art school?'

'You're only fourteen. Where could you possibly apply?'

'The drawing class at the Finnish Art Society!' Bigga jumped up and snatched the photo album. 'Besides, I'm nearly fifteen.'

'But Bigga-Marja, is it really the place for you...?'

Bigga-Marja gripped the album in her arms and glared at Inkeri. She had been expecting a rather different reaction. 'Do you remember when we went to the laying of the church foundations?'

'Yes, I do. You didn't want to put on your Sámi costume; you even wanted to throw your cap away.'

'Exactly!'

'There's no need to be ashamed of it.'

'That's not what I mean!'

'Then what *do* you mean?'

Bigga-Marja bit her lip, cast a glance at Olavi. Their eyes met in the reflection in the window. She turned back and looked at Inkeri.

'I mean, you only wanted me in the paper because of what you saw.'

'I don't follow.'

'You had an idealized image of what I am! And it's the same now too. First you rant about how we should go to school and get an education, but once we're in school, you want us all to be a certain way. That's why you want me to go to the Sámi college in Inari. You can't stand the idea that I'm not as magnificent and exotic as your African folk!' Bigga shouted, and threw the album to the floor. Some of the photographs came loose, their white edges protruding helplessly from beneath the covers.

Inkeri stood up briskly. 'What on earth are you talking about?'

'Give it a rest,' Bigga sulked, retreating to the sofa to sit down and look through the stamp collection. She opened it at a page where Piera had gathered stamps showing images of Lapland. Inkeri gave Olavi an almost panicked look. He shrugged his shoulders and didn't say anything. Instead, he turned and continued looking out at the bleak lake and the fell rising up behind it.

He saw a reflection in the window. *The rusted rumbling of the railway, iron against iron. Dead leaves.* Feathers gently floated down upon the body. It was strange how you could sense death before even smelling the air. Olavi closed his eyes.

He had been quick.

The first shot had missed.

And hit a bird.

The bird fell from the sky and made a surprisingly loud noise as it thumped against the earth. Its wings flailed in vain as it lay in the middle of the peat bog. Its throat let out a sound that the bird had never made before. The kind of sound you make only once in a lifetime. It was the sound of death.

It was then, at the latest, that the unsuspecting Heiskanen should have reached for his weapon, but he remained frozen on the spot. The memory of summer still lingered in the air. It was going to be a beautiful day. They both looked at the bird in confusion. He opened his mouth. After the second shot, darkness. Silence ringing in the ears.

He had killed another man. He had killed his friend Heiskanen. What kind of man kills his friend? He remembered the nearby marsh tea swaying in the wind, like a swan's wing. He wondered what Heiskanen had been trying to say. Perhaps he was about to ask for mercy. Could those final words have changed everything?

The only noise was the sound of Heiskanen's neck snapping as the bullet pierced his throat and gullet.

Blood spurted on to the tussocks, but its flow stopped quickly. His eyes glassed over into a final gaze.

As he dug the pit, he closed his eyes and tried to think of something else. The prisoners' washing routines; the way they were rounded up once a week in groups of ten and hosed down, just as one might wash a horse after sowing barley in the fields.

As he was about to leave, for the first time that day he felt the urge to empty his bladder. He had to try twice before anything came out.

It stung.

What might be causing it? Perhaps the dryness. The foreskin hung rough around the end of his penis and he pulled it to the side, tried again. Nothing happened. He tried counting to ten. The numbers carried weight. Too much weight.

It was already late evening when he finally returned to the camp. The guard at the gate asked where he had been. He had to give an account of his whereabouts to the command, but instead he walked straight back to the tent without seeing or doing anything. By the time he arrived at the tent, he was frozen, shivering, though inside it was hot as a furnace.

After crawling into bed, he immediately drifted into a delirious slumber, his mind racing with images of reindeer, midges, blood, gunshots. His entire body was tacky with sweat. He tried to take deep breaths, then exhale again. The mattresses creaked, and the beds beneath them. He curled up beneath the blankets, lay on his left side and pulled his right leg across his body. Seen from above, it would have looked as though he was running. He had placed his hands under the pillow to raise his head slightly. His right hand quivered next to his head.

In a calm voice, he murmured to himself the way you might whisper to a horse, a reindeer or some other timid creature. Soothingly. He had gathered the blanket into a bundle, placed it under his armpit and squeezed it the way he used to when he was a child, but not quite.

Suddenly, Inkeri dropped something on the floor and Olavi all but leapt into the air. Both Inkeri and Bigga looked at him, taken aback at his reaction, then glanced at each other. *It's all right, it's all right,* Olavi mumbled and looked at Bigga. They hadn't said a word since the events at the graveyard. Over the years, Olavi had asked Bigga all kinds of things. He had even asked her to spy for him. She had always told him whenever she learnt that Inkeri had acquired any new information or if she had seen Koskela. Bigga had taken his side, and he didn't deserve her loyalty. He wanted to know whether Inkeri's investigations were making progress.

'Marja?' Olavi asked, and moved next to her on the sofa. Before he and Koskela had gone their separate ways up on the fell, Koskela had shown him something. It was a diary. *His* diary. Koskela had shown it to him and asked if he could give it to Inkeri.

'How come you've still got that old thing?' Olavi gasped, and stroked the book's blue cover. He had almost missed it. There was a time when that diary was the only thing he could trust. It had never been taken away from him. Everything else had, but not that. But eventually he had handed it over to Koskela. Its contents were simply too much, too sensitive. Too many memories. There could be no evidence that the camp had ever existed.

'I thought you'd got rid of it. Like you planned.'

'No, Väinö, I didn't get rid of it. I plan to exchange this for the photograph. Inkeri deserves to know the truth, don't you think?' Koskela asked, and looked him in the eye. 'And when I do that, you know what it will mean. You'll have to leave unless you want to end up in prison.'

Olavi looked at the opened stamp collection. In one of the stamps, a small, dark-haired woman dressed in colourful clothing stood in front of a tepee. Bigga looked up at him.

'Yes?'

'Do you still have the ball?'

Bigga glanced first at Inkeri, then back at Olavi.

'What ball?'

'The cradle-ball.'

'Yes. Why?'

'Good. No reason. Just, good, that's all,' he said quietly. He lowered himself to the floor, picked up the photograph album and looked through the images. For a while he marvelled at how different they looked this close up. He closed the album, replaced it on the table, shut the door behind him.

The rusted rumbling of the railway, iron against iron. A signpost decaying in the mud. He couldn't make out the name, but he knew it already.

He had crossed the final frontier.

INARI

Sept. 1944

K OŚKELA CAME to visit me this morning and told me that there are riots everywhere. 'The border will soon pass over us,' he said as he packed my things into a bundle and helped me to my feet. He said he will help me to escape. 'Good God, man, you're burning hot.'

After that, he didn't say anything to anyone. He opened the door and showed his badge. He lifted me in his arms as though I were dead, carried me out of the door and didn't look back. We will never return.

Sept. 1944

Koskela gave me Saara's letter and told me that the host with whom she has been staying is the village ironsmith. Piera is his name, and he owns the smithy by the church. Piera, I say, tasting the name. And it is to a man by this name that Koskela is taking me now. Right away. We will be there soon.

Black-feathered birds sing in the fields in the bright of daybreak. When they take flight, the sky is like darkness itself.

Sept. 1944

We have already driven past Rovaniemi. There is unrest all around. I read Saara's letter again and again, so often that my heart could burst. She says that, if I will still have her, we can escape this dreadful place together. And that she will forgive me.

She tells me about a young girl, Hágas-Bierá Biggá-Márjá, who lives with her grandfather at the smithy. She writes about how well the two of them get on and says that, if she can, she will take the girl with us.

She explains that she may be forced to leave before I arrive, because her residence card has expired. I look at the ticket she gave Koskela and that he has given me. It is a ticket to America.

ENONTEKIÖ, 1950

THE MORNING had already warmed when Inkeri heard a knock at the inner door in the porch. Koskela stepped inside, bringing the fragrant summer's air with him. The mosquitoes buzzed along behind him, managing to get inside before he could close the door. Inkeri looked up from her book, puzzled. Bigga-Marja glanced at him from the sofa inquisitively.

'You decided to stay on for a while after the funeral?' Inkeri asked. Five days had passed since then.

Koskela got straight to the point. 'You wanted to know more about Väinö Remes. It looks like today is your lucky day.' He sat down at the table and placed his blue cap on its green surface. Inkeri stood up.

'Coffee?' she asked, and began absent-mindedly looking for the pot. She beckoned to Bigga, who came to help her. Koskela eyed up the room. The curtains were drawn across the windows. It was dim inside, almost dark. For a moment, he wondered why Inkeri kept the curtains closed in such beautiful weather, but he let the matter go. It was none of his business. He lit his pipe.

Inkeri took out the fine set of china, laid out cups and saucers for three and placed a jug of milk on the table.

'Do you remember when I told you about those prisoners? That people used to barter using the prisoners as currency? Well. Sometimes, some of those prisoners were sent to Poland.'

'Yes?'

'And we received a lot of prisoners from Poland too. It was all supposed to look like a standard exchange. The Finnish authorities were only too happy to trade Soviet prisoners for any of the distant Finnic peoples that the Nazis had picked up. In return, the Nazis took our Jews, Serbs, homosexuals, gypsies, and what have you.'

Inkeri sat down in her chair, placed a finger in front of her mouth and rubbed her lips. She fiddled with her box of cigarettes. The roasted aroma of coffee filled the room. Her head ached. A storm was coming, that must be why. When she closed her eyes and opened them again, for a moment she couldn't see anything at all.

'Go on.'

'The prisoners were used in exchange for other things too.'

'What do you mean?'

'Before the war, and even during the war, the Finnish authorities were developing the idea of… establishing a racial-biological research institute.'

'Like in Germany?'

'Just like in Germany.'

'Where doctors would examine…?'

'Racial characteristics. The institute's most important task would be to drive population policy in the new Greater Finland and to prevent the procreation of any undesirable elements. The programme's developer, Niilo Pesonen, was a popular figure in Nazi Germany. And he became acquainted with many of the camp commanders in Finland too.' Koskela wet his lips and considered his next words carefully. In his hands he held a book. The diary.

'What we know is that a Committee for Racial Purity was formed to take the matter further. In addition, the programme received funding to conduct physical anthropological research which involved examining the bodies of Finns and other related peoples. To this end, the war provided the perfect preconditions. Throughout the war, this Dr Pesonen had bodies sent to the anatomy department of the University of Helsinki. Mostly those of Karelians and Ingrians. There might have been some others too.'

'Isn't that illegal?' Inkeri gasped.

'It certainly is. Pesonen was eventually convicted of mutilating bodies or incitement to mutilate bodies, or something similar,' Koskela explained. 'Before the end of the war, the committee destroyed all their documents. Everyone known to have been involved with the committee burnt all correspondence with race experts in Germany. Even personal diaries and calendars suddenly disappeared. This is why it has been impossible to investigate the matter further. That photograph of yours... It is one of the few documents that could be used as evidence.'

'But why...?' Inkeri sighed. 'Why did they do that?'

'I'm sure we both know why,' said Koskela, almost amused. 'The intention was to gather more information on the Finnish race.'

Inkeri lowered her eyes. 'Are you suggesting that bodies from these camps were sent away for research?' she asked.

'I'm not suggesting anything. Everything I've told you is mere speculation, it's unofficial information, and I don't know anything about it. I repeat: I do not know anything. But, if this did indeed happen, the task of acquiring the bodies was given to a certain Finn working at the camp in Inari. This turned out to be a mutually very beneficial collaboration. For the Nazis, this was the most desirable outcome, though it was harder to provide bodies from the Finnish camps because the practice was considered ethically questionable.'

'What has this got to do with my husband?' Inkeri asked impatiently.

Koskela sighed. Inkeri looked fretfully at him, then at Bigga, who had raised her eyebrows and appeared to be listening intently.

'It's my understanding that your husband struck some kind of deal at the camp. It's possible that he was helping to divert bodies to the research institute, and in return he received better treatment and conditions at the camp. I can attest that Kaarlo had preferential treatment at the Inari camp. Highly preferential.'

Inkeri could no longer say anything. She thought of her husband. She simply could not believe such a thing of Kalle—ever.

'When people panic, they change,' Koskela continued quietly, as if sensing Inkeri's pending questions. 'None of us can predict how we will behave under such duress. None of us knows the limits of our endurance, we don't know when or how we will break. But everybody breaks eventually, it's just a question of time.' His voice was calm and steady. Inkeri suddenly felt immensely sad. She clenched her hands in her lap. Still she could not speak.

'Towards the end of the war, the Nazis became suspicious of us Finns. And with good reason. They started building fortifications all over Lapland in case of a Finnish offensive. On top of that, there was a very significant risk that the Finnish prisoners or the Finns who had worked at the camps would start talking about what they had seen. I believe this is the reason your husband was to be transferred to another camp, where he would likely have been executed.'

Koskela tried to find the right words to continue. '*Väinö Remes…*' he began. Inkeri sat up straight. 'It was late August when Väinö Remes was sent to hospital. At first, I thought there must have been a partisan attack. Instead, I learnt that Väinö had been instructed to shoot someone. His colleague. At the camp commander's orders. It pushed Remes over the edge. In fact, he might have started to lose his grip on reality long before this. In any case, he woke up in the hospital.'

Koskela paused. He took out his pipe, began calmly filling it. 'At that point, we all knew the war would soon come to an end. And it wasn't going to end in our favour. We were all in danger. Me, Väinö, Saara and Kaarlo. At this point, Kaarlo was still in jail. My jail, and that meant he was my problem. Eventually, I decided it was best to bring Saara and Kalle down here to safety. From here, it would be easier to cross the border into Sweden or head up to the Norwegian coast, where they could get on a Red Cross ship bound for America. I knew a man here who could take people across the fells to safety. Needless to say, that man was Piera,' said Koskela, and glanced at Bigga-Marja, who raised an eyebrow but remained silent. Of course, she knew all of this already.

'What happened then?' asked Inkeri.

'Kaarlo was brought here. Piera set off across the fells to take him and a small group of others to safety. Officially, I registered Kaarlo as having arrived at the Enontekiö camp, but by this point, who was counting the prisoners any more?' he said with a dull laugh. 'It's ironic that it was my registration in the prisoner log that brought you up here in the first place,' he said, and looked at his cap. 'Well, it wasn't you that worked it out. It was someone else, right?' Koskela looked Inkeri in the eye. She blushed.

'Piera? So he helped Kaarlo escape? Why did nobody say anything until now?'

'There was nothing to say,' Koskela replied, and shrugged his shoulders. 'Piera helped a great many people escape. I doubt he even knew your husband's name; he might have forgotten ever meeting him. You see, not everything Piera did was strictly legal. During the Lapland War, he never left the village, despite the order to evacuate, but remained up in the fells doing things that might be beneficial both to the Finns and to the Nazis. If these activities had come to light, Piera would have been hauled up in front of a tribunal. At the very least, he would have been interrogated, and there was a danger he might have exposed us all.'

'Áddjá would never expose anybody!' Bigga-Marja shouted. They both turned to look at her. Koskela gave a warm chuckle.

'You're right there, Bigga-Marja. I didn't mean he would have revealed our names. No. But there are many ways to give up a person's identity. One careless description, say, a person's habit of twiddling a cigarette between his lips, could reveal everything,' he explained, standing up and walking over to the coffee pot. He poured a cup for Inkeri and one for himself.

Inkeri frowned. 'Did Kaarlo escape?' she asked. 'If he's still alive, why… Why hasn't he tried to contact me?' she gulped, trying to conceal her astonishment, her disappointment. Koskela returned to his chair. He patted his pocket, then took out a pile of folded papers.

'I've asked you before, but I'll ask you again. Have you ever wondered why somebody is helping you to find him?'

'You mean, why are *you* helping me?'

Koskela chortled. 'That's a good question too. But the person who passed you this information. Has it ever crossed your mind that someone else might want to find your husband too?'

'What do you mean?'

'As I explained, his treatment at the camp was exceptional. Nobody is just given a position like that; you have to earn it. He earned his position by agreeing to sign certain documents. Documents that, if they had come to light in the wrong circumstances or at the wrong time, would have caused problems for lots of people. And so, the signatory to those documents had to be someone who could be sacrificed if necessary, whose existence didn't matter one way or the other.'

Inkeri stared at him, unable to fathom what she was hearing. Koskela sighed and slid the papers across the table.

'Here. Do you see?' he said, and pointed at a document that looked like a list of prisoner details. Name, weight, age, race. The list was clearly only a fragment of a larger document, but the signature at the bottom of the page was penned in a comforting, familiar hand: *Kaarlo Lindqvist*.

'I…' Inkeri gasped.

'Is this your husband's handwriting?' Koskela asked pointedly.

'Yes… yes…' She picked up the piece of paper and squinted, the better to read it.

'No, you mustn't touch them. You have never seen these papers. Now do you understand? *This* is why your contacts want to help you. They are looking for your husband. They know he has signed these documents. My guess is that they managed to unearth copies of some of these lists before the racial purity committee had a chance to burn everything. And the person helping you was an agent with the Paatsalo Unit during the war.'

Inkeri flinched.

'Exactly. Some of the agents are still continuing their investigation. To them, you are just a marionette,' said Koskela in a low voice, looking her right in the eye. Inkeri sat down, dumbfounded.

'If Kaarlo is alive, this is why he cannot contact you. It might land you in trouble too,' he continued. Inkeri closed her eyes.

'I need that photograph,' he said.

'What?'

'The photograph, the one you showed me. I need it. If it falls into the wrong hands, many people will be in trouble. Innocent people. Kaarlo too. Your husband.'

Inkeri said nothing.

Koskela tilted his head to one side. 'I'm prepared to give you something in return. Something that will tell you more about your husband than you might wish to know. You remember I told you that some of the soldiers kept a diary?'

Inkeri nodded.

'I have a diary for you. It belongs to Väinö Remes. Will you exchange the photograph for that? Inkeri?'

She could not speak. She was so profoundly confused about everything she had heard. Her eyes hurt more than usual, as though tiny electric shocks were coursing through them. Her head was throbbing.

'But how does Olavi fit into all this?' she stammered. Koskela looked up to the ceiling and smiled. Bigga kept her mouth firmly shut. Koskela took his last sip of coffee, placed his cap on his head.

'If you recall, I told you that the task of sorting the bodies was given to one of the Finns at the camp.'

'Yes. Wasn't it Väinö Remes?'

'No,' said Koskela. 'It was Olavi Heiskanen.'

It was impossible to read Inkeri's expression. Bigga sat utterly motionless. Koskela stood up, placed the notebook on the table. On its cover were the words: *Väinö Remes, Diary*. He stared at it long and hard.

'I've discussed the matter with Olavi. He gave me permission to give you this,' he said quietly. 'You might find some comfort in it. I can't give you anything else. But now, I implore you, for your own sake, for Olavi's sake, for Kaarlo's sake: don't look into this any further. And do not speak about it. In this matter, I'm afraid you can't trust anybody, not even your childhood friend. So, I repeat: do not look into this any further. Ever again,' he said, then left the notebook on the table and picked up the photograph, which Inkeri had quietly slid in front of him.

ROVANIEMI–MUONIO

Sept. 1944

I HAVE ONLY JUST realized that the belongings Koskela
fetched for me are not in fact my belongings. I pointed this
out to him. This must be the wrong bundle, I said, told him that
these are Olavi Heiskanen's things, and that Olavi Heiskanen
was lying dead at the side of the winter route to Hyljelahti.
'Now they are yours,' he said. When I asked where my passport
was, Koskela replied that he had burnt it.

'You can't hunt down a dead man. And you can't imprison
a dead man either,' he said. 'What you did might have been
at Felde's command, but I have a feeling that command will
be worthless before long.' I held the discharge papers in my
hand and looked at Heiskanen's picture, which had clearly
been cut from a larger photograph. 'But I don't look anything
like him,' I said.

'It's an old photograph, I'll grant you, and in bad condition,
but it'll do for your purposes. From now on, you are Olavi
Heiskanen, nobody else. Remember that. Only the dead can
be truly free,' said Koskela. 'You cannot imprison a dead man.
Say it. Start your new life. Say your name!' he ordered me.

And I said it. 'My name is Olavi Heiskanen.'

Sept. 1944

The fires have already started. Koskela says that soon, once the war turns against us, the Nazis will burn everything to the ground. 'That's for sure,' he said. 'And you can be certain that in those blazes a few species will end up extinct.' He glanced at the alpine rhododendron in my hands.

Saara once said that we exist between life and death and that we are merely waiting for an impetus, just a tiny impulse, something to jolt us in one direction or another. Forwards. We either die or we live.

ENONTEKIÖ, 1950

INKERI LOOKED at the cross in the church. A week earlier, the altarpiece had been erected. It had arrived in three pieces and depicted the wintry, Lappish landscape: a convoy of reindeer was making its way across the fells, and in front of the reindeer stood a man and woman in Sámi attire. Inkeri turned and looked at Bigga-Marja. The girl was only standing a few metres away. Matilda the pig was lying next to her, seemingly without a care in the world. Bigga fiddled with the cradle-ball in her muddy hands.

'Is it good now?' asked Inkeri, and Bigga-Marja nodded. They had decided to plant Olavi's alpine rhododendron and let it flower. Bigga had dug a hole. This was a good place, the right place. They had chosen the most shaded spot in an area next to the churchyard—right where the prison camp used to be. Bigga glanced at Inkeri and nodded. They both lowered their heads in a moment's silence.

In recent weeks, they had spent most of their time together. Bigga had moved into the house, and once she turned fifteen at the beginning of July, she reminded Inkeri of Melander's promise to hire her. Inkeri had sent the newspaper editor photographs from the album that Bigga had put together back in the spring. It had made a real impression on him. Or perhaps not. In any case, Bigga now received payment for the jobs she did. Now she was officially Inkeri's assistant. Meanwhile, Inkeri found it increasingly hard to regain her touch with the camera. Bigga now took almost all the photographs and developed them herself, while Inkeri lay at home in bed, her eyes aching. She took two cigarettes from her packet, handed one to Bigga and took the other for herself. She lit them, her hand trembling faintly. She had become old.

'All done?' she asked.

'Yes. All done,' said Bigga with a nod.

As soon as Koskela had left, it dawned on them that Olavi had disappeared without saying a word. It had been a month already, and it seemed quite certain that he wasn't coming back. At first it had felt strange, the idea of not having Olavi around any longer. Nobody knew where he had gone or where he would end up. Inkeri had tried to ask Koskela whether Olavi had been arrested or imprisoned. According to Koskela, this wasn't the case, though nobody knew for certain. Olavi had left Bigga-Marja a large sum of money, but with no accompanying letter. Just money, rolled up and placed on her desk with a small note: *Piera left you this.* Bigga-Marja took the money, looked around Olavi's room and sat down on his bed, then eventually she told Inkeri everything she knew.

In late August 1944, when Piera had set off to guide Kaarlo across the fells to safety, Saara had remained in their house. *In this very room*, said Bigga. A few weeks later, a warrant was issued for Saara's arrest. Piera and Matilda the pig had returned home the previous day, and Bigga-Marja was surprised to see Saara packing up her belongings in the attic room. She would always remember the sounds, the way the floor creaked under Saara's footsteps. In the early hours of the morning, with a small bag slung over her shoulder, Saara told her that a Finnish soldier was coming here—to look for her.

'*Bahás olmmái?*' Bigga had asked. Saara smiled warmly. They had become like sisters, though the time they had spent together was all too short.

'No, he's not a bad man,' Saara replied, and stepped up to Bigga-Marja, hugged her. When Bigga had asked where she was going, Saara looked back at her with a smile. 'I'm going where the rhododendrons flower,' she laughed with a flippant wave of the hand. 'There's a Red Cross ship setting sail from the Norwegian coast. It's heading to North America,' she explained, then smiled the way people with happy secrets smile.

'But before I go, I want to give you this. It's the most precious thing I have. It will help you to safety, just as it helped me to safety.' Saara then placed a small clinking object in the girl's hand.

'And you can tell the man who comes here that I have something for him, and that I've taken it to the prison camp. Tell him to go there and fetch it. Tell him it's a ticket to freedom, in case he decides to stay here and not to follow me.'

'A ticket to freedom? Why can't you just leave it here?'

'Because the police might raid the house,' Saara explained gravely. 'It's safer there.' Without even noticing, Bigga had begun following Saara out of the house and started badgering to know what was in the parcel.

'It's a picture. A photograph. Some people would do anything with information like this. If you know how to read it properly, it will tell you lots of things.'

'Like what?' Bigga asked curiously. They had already passed the well and the dead tree, the crossroads, the old church. Saara looked at the girl and smiled. 'You're too young to understand.'

'Grown-ups always say that! It's so annoying!'

Saara laughed gently. 'A photograph is just an image. But it can tell you a lot if you know how to read it. And a person who knows how to take photographs might one day be able to share information that could change the world,' said Saara, lifting up the metal tin. 'And this tin contains one such photograph.'

When they were halfway to the camp, Bigga turned back. She could no longer remember why. No, she did remember. Matilda had been following them snuffling loudly, and at one point she bit Bigga. She had to take the pig back home. She and Saara agreed to meet again outside the camp before her ride arrived.

Five or ten minutes later, Bigga heard an explosion.

None of them could have known that the Germans had already begun to evacuate the camp and execute the prisoners. Neither could they have known that they would destroy the camp complex with explosives, that everything would go up in flames and all around them would lie the bodies of charred animals, dead people, the taste and smell of iron.

The force of the blast knocked Bigga-Marja to the ground. The pig was terrified and was making such high-pitched squeals that Bigga had to hold her hands over her ears. All around there was smoke. The explosion felt warm, like an embrace. Everything was ablaze. In her mouth, she caught the taste of blood and life. And death.

How could someone be so present one moment, then disappear the next? Just like that?

A few days after the explosion, Olavi arrived. In Koskela's car.

When Bigga told him, Ovllá couldn't believe what had happened to Saara, he refused to believe it, though he went immediately to the camp. Saara's body was never found, not even burnt remains. Bigga-Marja was still nothing but a child, so maybe she had misremembered, maybe she had seen wrong; that's what Olavi told himself.

But he did find the tin containing the photograph. Lying in the dirt beside it was a small silver lighter, the one bearing the inscription *Saara*.

And the birds. They simply disappeared. All at once. They only returned the following winter. The migratory birds from Africa were the first to arrive, Áddjá told her. Áddjá knew lots of things. Áddjá had seen the world.

Then came the rest of the birds.

And the following year, the same birds came back again, and this time they stayed.

Inkeri had thought of Bigga's story almost daily. Perhaps Saara's absence was the one thing that had kept Olavi here all these years. Perhaps Inkeri and Olavi had something in common after all.

Inkeri looked at the dew as it glistened in the churchyard, like diamonds or stars. Inkeri and Bigga-Marja caught each other's eye. They linked hands, stood by the flower a moment longer, then turned away. Matilda remained by the church. They had both decided that the pig could live freely now, but every night she always came back to the house, and Bigga or Inkeri locked her in the pen. Out of habit more than anything.

Inkeri felt the gentle breeze against her face. The light lingered in their hair for a moment, on their skin, until clouds hid the sun from view. Inkeri closed her eyes and saw a sky filled with the silhouettes of M-shaped birds. She opened her eyes and saw the fell. As time passed, she thought less and less of Kaarlo. She imagined him as somehow different from before. She decided that he had caught that boat after all, travelled to Brazil or somewhere else in South America. That he would see exotic places and countries and forget about the past. She would never know for sure, but that's what she had decided. It was the only way she could move on in her own life. And she had chosen life. She heard the call of a bird and caught the scent of fresh earth. The late-summer's morning turned to mist against the northern sky. The sun, climbing ever higher, pierced a cloud, making it sparkle. The light was beautiful. Despite the pain it caused, it brought her comfort.

At some point that summer, Bigga-Marja had persistently asked what Inkeri planned to do with the house. She had finally made a decision. She planned to open a bookshop selling the kind of books that people actually wanted to read around here. In all languages, Sámi, Finnish, Norwegian. And she wanted to open a photography studio. She had already asked Bigga-Marja if she would like to work as a photographer—which she did.

Once they arrived back at the garden, Inkeri sat down on the front steps and Bigga went off to fetch water from the well. Inkeri had finished reading Väinö Remes's diary. Pages had been torn out here and there, words scored out. *It's been redacted*, Koskela explained when he paid a visit, brought some flowers for the vase on the table and, with a look of concern, whispered something to Bigga near the woodshed. It was Inkeri they were worried about. She looked at the sky. Bigga approached her. Perhaps it was a bird, perhaps something else, or perhaps nothing that finally broke the silence between them.

'The birds are getting ready to fly south,' she said. A bullfinch and a jackdaw seemed to be having a disagreement. The titmice were singing. The birds appeared to be bathing in a large ant-heap. Beneath the window, the white marsh tea swayed in the breeze.

'Áddjá used to say that travel is the most miraculous thing in the world.'

'It is,' Inkeri laughed. 'Though I have a feeling your grandfather meant a different kind of travel.'

Bigga looked contemplative. She gazed up at Inkeri.

'I managed to fix the colour camera. We can try using it to take our next passport photographs or some pictures for the magazine,' said Inkeri. The girl smiled and sat down next to her. Inkeri took a cigarette from her pocket, then the silver lighter, and handed them to Bigga.

'Marja,' she whispered. The wind almost snatched the word away. Throughout the summer, she realized that she had started to see the world differently. She noticed how abundant it was, how diverse, and quietly accepted that her life, her hopes and dreams had never been dependent on the light after all. She had simply decided so.

Inkeri finally took off her sunglasses and looked Bigga-Marja right in the eye.

'What is it, Inkeri?' she asked.

'Tell me about your Lapland.'

ENONTEKIÖ

Sept. 1944

THE WAR is over.

Translator's Afterword

It goes without saying that complex, sprawling global conflicts like the Second World War were experienced in different ways by different people in different places. In Britain, for instance, there is a particular narrative of how we think of the war, and this is underpinned by the language we use to talk about it. Events like the Blitz, the Normandy landings and the Dunkirk evacuations don't require any explanation for English-language readers because they are so ingrained in our collective, supra-generational memory of the war. However, when faced with similarly iconic Second World War events from the Finnish context—say, the destruction and subsequent reconstruction of Lapland—an amount of background and context is needed. And whereas our gallery of protagonists from Churchill to Vera Lynn and the Bletchley codebreakers needs no introduction, readers may be less familiar with their Finnish equivalents Marshal C.G.E. Mannerheim (a prominent military leader and subsequent President of Finland), Risto Ryti (wartime prime minister and later president), the Lotta Brigade (a voluntary women's auxiliary organization) and the Paatsalo Unit (a collective of double agents working reconnaissance operations along Finland's north-eastern border during the war).

Naturally, Finland has its own unique narrative of the Second World War too. In fact, Finns consider the war as at least three separate conflicts: the Winter War (1939–40), the Continuation War (1941–44) and the Lapland War (1944–45), and it is during the two latter conflicts and their aftermath that the events of *Land of Snow and Ashes* take place. It follows, therefore, that Finnish has its own vocabulary to discuss themes associated with these conflicts, and rendering this intricate discourse in another language without footnotes, while maintaining the elegance of the original prose, is a challenge for the translator.

Much has been written on Finland's role in the Second World War, but to provide brief context for the events of this novel, during the Continuation War Finland aligned itself with Nazi Germany because both had a shared enemy in the Soviet Union. Though still a taboo subject in Finland, there was an expansionist aspect to the Continuation War. One of its goals, advanced primarily by the Finnish nationalist organizations the Academic Karelia Society and the Patriotic People's Movement, and at least notionally supported by former President P.E. Svinhufvud, was the creation of a so-called Greater Finland. Finland's eastern border had already been redrawn several times since 1809, so the aim of Greater Finland was to incorporate all the Finnic peoples living on the Russian side of the border (including Karelians, Ingrians and various Sámi-speaking communities) back into the Finnish fatherland. As the novel lays bare, the matter of deciding who could be considered ethnically 'pure' came perilously close to full-blown eugenics, as the references to the doctor, anthropologist and 'race researcher' Yrjö Kajava suggest. Needless to say, after the war the cause of, and the ideology behind, a Greater Finland were swiftly disavowed.

The Continuation War came to an end with the signing on 19th September 1944 of the Moscow Armistice, the template for the eventual peace treaty between Finland and Russia. As well as ceding many areas along the eastern border back to Russia, including the Petsamo region in eastern Lapland, the armistice also required that Finland eject all German troops from its territory. As they retreated from Lapland, the Germans sought to destroy as much infrastructure as possible and planted innumerable landmines—as one iconic road sign put it, 'Als Dank für *nicht* bewiesene Waffenbrüderschaft' ('By way of thanks for *not* showing brotherhood in arms'). The scorched earth withdrawal from the region saw thousands of houses and churches razed to the ground and hundreds of roads and bridges detonated. This period was known as the Lapland War, and it is in the lead-up to this shift in allegiance between Finland, Germany and Russia that Väinö's diary is written. Inkeri's arrival in Enontekiö in 1947 coincides with the initial phase of the post-war reconstruction.

Meanwhile, the rebuilding of Lapland provided a suitable opportunity to continue the process of assimilating the Sámi into Finnish life and culture. This process has been going on since at least the seventeenth century with the imposition of Christianity and the Church's active discouragement of local beliefs and religious practices, shamanistic traditions such as *yoik*-singing, and the speaking of Sámi languages. As the novel describes, not only were schools rebuilt after the war, education in Lapland was entirely restructured, for instance by making children 'board' at school dormitories, far away from their families and traditions, and teaching them Finnish instead of their native Sámi languages. At the time of events in the novel the Sámi began to express growing resentment at their treatment, and to this day there is a sense that each new law passed represents the slow erosion of their centuries-old traditions and livelihoods. This long-held grudge is encapsulated in Piera's untranslatable apophthegm 'Lanta sikenee, Lappi pakenee', literally 'the nation tightens its grip, Lapland retreats'. I have rendered this on p. 94 as 'the south prospers while the north withers'. Framing this as a conflict between north and south is, of course, a slight oversimplification; it is more a case of one culture gradually encroaching upon another over a period of centuries. The character of Bigga-Marja embodies this clash; her double-barrelled name is half Sámi, half Finnish, and, caught between the two cultures, she struggles to establish her own identity.

The question of how to refer to the Sámi in English is complicated, as we lack the words to express subtle distinctions between the groups and identities that are the focus of *Land of Snow and Ashes*. In her 1967 book *The Finns and Their Country*, Wendy Hall writes that 'the Lapps are to be distinguished from the Laplanders, who are Finns living in the province of Lapland'. The Finnish term *lappalainen* ('Lapp') is today considered somewhat pejorative, though it appears frequently in the language of the novel. Because Hall's distinction is important for the interpersonal dynamics at play in the novel, throughout this translation I use 'Sámi' and 'Lapp' to refer to specifically Sámi characters (e.g. Piera and Bigga-Marja) and 'Finn', 'Laplander' and occasionally 'southerner' to refer to the non-Sámi characters (e.g. Inkeri and Olavi).

This being said, the Sámi themselves are far from a homogenous group. There are at least nine main Sámi languages, including Northern Sámï, Akkala Sámi (now virtually extinct) and Inari Sámi, which are all mentioned in the novel. Furthermore, as nomadic people the Sámi have never been confined within the arbitrary borders of nation states, though the constant redrawing of these borders has created many problems over the years, particularly for reindeer herders. The Sámi still consider their land to encompass the entire area from the Norwegian coast in the west all the way to the Kola Peninsula in the east. As one of the herdsmen in the novel notes, 'The reindeer bow to the authority of no man.'

Though, to this day, there are Sámi news broadcasts every evening on national television, Finnish and Northern Sámi, the largest of the Sámi languages and the one used most frequently in this novel, are not mutually intelligible. For this reason I have elected to retain examples of Sámi languages in their original forms, not in a voyeuristic attempt to provide local colour but to preserve the sense of alienation that Finnish readers would experience when reading these passages. The snippets of dialogue in Sámi, notably the encounter with the herdsman, serve to put the reader in Inkeri's shoes: though she represents the 'dominant' culture, she can't understand anything of the local language. As Piera puts it, she will always be an outsider. When they read this passage, Finnish readers are at a loss too: no Finnish translation is provided for these dialogues, and though Finnish readers will readily identify the language as Sámi, they won't understand more than a word here and there. This communication barrier—between Finns and the Sámi and between the reader and the text—in fact exemplifies the cultural clash explored throughout the novel.

As I write these words in Hanko, the southernmost point in mainland Finland, it is worth remembering that from here it is over 1,200 kilometres to Inari. Finland is a vast country, and even to readers here in the south, Lapland is both geographically, linguistically and culturally a distant, alluring place that most people have never visited. I hope this short afterword will help open a window into the fascinating history and culture that informs the world of *Land of Snow and Ashes*.

DAVID HACKSTON

Hanko, July 2021

Acknowledgements

The author wishes to thank the following people and organizations: Aleksi Pöyry, Suvi Vaarla, Pirita Näkkäläjärvi, Oula-Antti Labba, Pirita Palismaa, Oula Seitsonen, Anna Louhensalo, Iiris Aaltonen, and everybody else who has helped and supported me. Your input has been invaluable. Thank you to my publisher Otava for the support and trust you have shown me. The completion of this book was generously supported by the Otava Book Foundation, Nuoren Voiman Liitto (the Villa Sarkia residence), and the North Savo Regional Fund of the Finnish Cultural Foundation.